Draw Forth

How to Host Your Own Visual Conversations Without Having to Be a Professional Artist or a Full-On Facilitator

JEANNEL KING

Also by Jeannel King

What You Draw Is Good Enough (eBook)

Draw Forth

How to Host Your Own Visual Conversations
Without Having to Be a Professional Artist or a Full-On Facilitator

JEANNEL KING

Papumiho Press

Papumiho Press
8885 Rio San Diego Drive, Suite 237
San Diego, CA 92108

Illustrations: Jeannel King
Book Design: DesignGood + DesignGood Studio
Cover Design: DesignGood + DesignGood Studio
Photographs of Jeannel King: Rob Andrew

Library of Congress Control Number: 2014954071

First printing, November 2014
ISBN 978-0-9907864-0-5
Printed in the United States

10 9 8 7 6 5 4 3 2 1

This book is dedicated to visual conversationalists *everywhere* who are drawing out ideas while drawing forth the best in ourselves and each other. You rock!

Contents

Author's Note

I wasn't born with a marker in my hand, drawing conversations while wearing diapers. Heck, I never thought I could draw particularly well in the first place. My mom and younger sister were the artists in my family. While my sister drew super-cool freehand drawings, I took pads of tracing paper and copied other people's drawings before adding my unique embellishments to these basic forms.

Although I didn't view myself as an artist, I do remember the first time I stumbled into drawing a visual conversation. It was in Mrs. Schulz's fifth-grade class during my first-ever presentation. Each student had to present on a particular subject, and I got "alchemy."

Alchemy? What the heck was that? I went to the library (this was during the days before Google and the Internet) and dug up everything I could on the subject. I skimmed one book after another, fascinated by the idea of being able to transmute one substance into another. I was drawn in by the potential of finding universal cures for the things that ail us and by the possibility of giving something additional life. I dove into alchemy with the excitement of an explorer discovering a whole new world I never knew existed.

When the day came for our presentations, I was ready. I bounced in my seat as my classmates and I listened to student after student present various aspects of medieval history. Finally, it was time for the last speaker—me! I stood up at the front of the classroom, all frizzy-curly red hair and knobby knees. I set the stage for what alchemy was and what medieval alchemists sought to do.

"Now let me show you how they thought it could work," I said turning to the blackboard, picking up a piece of chalk and beginning to draw. All my research flowed out of me as I drew like a crazy person, connecting different alchemists' theories and ideas, displaying formulas for creating a philosopher's stone, what ideas got stolen from whom and who got killed for their ideas . . .

\>>RING!!!!!!!<<

I stopped, aghast. The class had ended, and I was not yet done with my presentation! I stood looking at the teacher, not sure what to do next. Mrs. Schultz called out that the class was dismissed; however, those interested in hearing the rest of my presentation could stay. The class erupted in a flurry of kids stuffing books into knapsacks and feet running, but when the dust settled a quarter of the class was still there! Not at their desks, but up with me by the chalkboard! One kid asked, "What about the gold? How'd they make the gold?"

I continued drawing and sharing what I learned. Then Mrs. Schultz said, "Well, this ties back into what you said about the very first alchemist." To my amazement, she picked up a piece of chalk and drew a connection between what I had first drawn at the start of my presentation and the new piece of information we had added!

Then another kid picked up a piece of chalk and said, "Yeah, but didn't that guy get killed for believing this?" And he drew a dude with "x" eyes and a dagger in his chest. With a few chalk marks, the visual conversation was on its way. Together we transformed something common into something special—we created visual alchemy!

Then, as can often happen, I went on with life and everything I wanted to "become," and my fifth grade drawing experience faded to memory. Following my passion for making a difference in the lives of people and their environment, I set about building a career working in nonprofit management.

Unfortunately, I sustained a work injury along the way that left my dominant arm permanently disabled, forcing me to modify how I worked. Realizing the standard writing modifications did not work for me, I took to the whiteboard in my office and the ease of using wider markers. At first, I would write out everything I had to do on the board. Then I would draw little flowers or swirls in the corners because, well, it was in my office, and I had to look at it. Besides, it did not matter if what I drew looked messed up: it was for me and I could always erase it and draw something else!

I cannot remember when it happened, but after a while something shifted in my brain. I had a blinding flash of the obvious: instead of writing stuff out on the whiteboard, I could just draw it! Letting my drawing do the heavy lifting, I would draw out the things I managed and write comments only as needed. It was awesome!

Other members of my management team started showing up in my office saying, "Hey, we need to start doing our meetings like THIS!" In a moment, my visual thinking moved from the office to the conference room and ultimately to the facilities we managed, working visually with the line staff and the consumers we served. It was not until I took an executive position in an environmental conservation nonprofit that worked with communities in Hawaii, Japan and Mexico that I realized drawing out ideas worked better to bypass language barriers and communicate ideas.

After leaving the nonprofit sector in 2009, I started helping people and organizations facilitate visual meetings and community events. The concept caught on like wildfire and in 2010 I launched my own business. It has been full-time from the start, and I have never looked back!

Today, I am a Stick Figure Strategist®, designing and facilitating complex conversations and strategies with simple drawings. Over the years I have drawn out ideas with formative organizations, Fortune 500 companies, and everything in between. From business brainstorming sessions to tech think tanks, community conversations to Commando vision quests, my markers and I have drawn out ideas while drawing forth the best in teams.

As experience has taught me, anyone (yes, this includes you!) can visually communicate ideas and connect with people in the process. Just imagine being able to jump into ANY conversation or engage your family, friends or team to draw forth their best thinking. You may not yet realize this, but you already have this power within you. It is just waiting to be drawn out.

This is what I am here for! Consider me your visual conversation coach. I am going to share a simple process with you to help you understand and use this visual language. Plus, I will provide you with plenty of practice opportunities along the way, so you can build your skills, become fluent and create your own visual alchemy.

Quite a few years have passed since I was in Mrs. Schultz's class; yet, this fifth-grade lesson stayed with me. Visual conversations continue to be my alchemy, and this book is my philosopher's stone. Thank you for allowing me to share it with you. I cannot wait to see what you draw forth with it!

PART 1:
Getting Ready

The Case for Visual Conversation

Remember learning a second language, for example French, German or Spanish, in junior high or high school? Perhaps you even took on learning another language in college, or as an adult. Invariably, you had to learn basic phrases asking people their name, how to get to the airport, or even something as esoteric as complimenting the local fishmonger on the quality of his fish. Well, visual conversation is just like learning a second language. The only difference is we are taking a conversational approach to learning this particular language, making it practical and useful.

It is one thing to be able to craft perfect sentences in another language so you can chat with our proverbial fishmonger. (This is why we all learn to speak a second language, right? Not!) It is another thing—and infinitely more useful—to actually COMMUNICATE your needs and desires to another person, to understand what they say

in return and to use this information effectively and well. This is why I am an advocate for visual conversations: their infinite usefulness and applicability.

We all innately have a visual second language. Chances are you just don't think of it as a language you can communicate with or may not be particularly skilled communicating in. Just like high school French, German or Spanish, if you don't use it, you lose it.

Most of us don't use it because our society has not made it universally okay to doodle in class, to draw out ideas, or to pick up the pen and draw things at work or during meetings.[1] As a result, your visual second language atrophies. The good news is it is still in there and probably stronger than the high school Spanish you may sometimes draw upon! In this Visual Age, visual knowledge finds a home in our brains long before junior high or high school.[2]

I am here to help you draw on and develop the skill set that allows you to jump into ANY visual conversation—not just one with the elusive fishmonger! The process I have crafted empowers you to engage your family, friends or team to draw forth their best thinking.

The tools and practices that follow will have anyone you work with on the same page as you from the start. People will feel seen and heard during your conversations, and you will be able to capture all the great "juice" that flows forth without losing or spilling a drop. Tapping into your visual conversationalist skills will allow you to more clearly express and explain ideas to others, so they can really see what you mean, understand the importance of it and even be inspired to take action!

As your visual conversation coach, I am going to share with you easy processes for understanding visual language and provide you with plenty of practice opportunities along the way to help you build your skills. Just as with any new or rusty language, in order to become conversational, you need to use it consistently and well. Use it or lose it, as they say!

So let's get started exploring the idea of conversation itself, through the eyes of three different people.

Three People, Three Different Conversations

Meet Alli, Pops and Becks!

Alli is Vice President of Innovation of Innovation for a global solutions company. As the person responsible for creating a culture of innovation within her company, she asked me to teach her how to draw out conversations with her C-Suite colleagues. Alli needs to be able to explain her ideas to people quickly, efficiently and in a way they can easily share with others, see themselves as a part of, believe in and buy into.

Pops is the Director of Student Affairs for an international university. While he can inspire people to consider new goals and possibilities for their future, he did not feel like he was able to bring his team "all the way." Pops wanted to help them visualize the steps they could take to achieve their goals, and more importantly, help them to believe they had what it took to make their goals a reality!

Becks is a Business Marketing Consultant working with clients who not only need to understand their marketing goals, but also complex concepts and strategies they have created together. It was important to Becks that her clients be able to implement their goals, ideas and strategies to achieve their desired results.

As you will see, even though Alli, Pops and Becks hold different roles in diverse industries, they can all apply these visual conversation techniques to engage their teams more effectively and get better results moving forward. More importantly, they don't have to be talented artists or certified facilitators; they can get the same great results at any skill level.

4 Things Every Visual Conversationalist Has In Common

Let's take a moment to look at the four things all visual conversationalists have in common (no matter what hat you wear), through the eyes of Alli, Pops and Becks:

1. Visual conversationalists engage in important, high-stakes conversations on a daily basis.

Sure, the stakes may be relative to the people involved in the conversation, but they are important nonetheless!

Does our company culture reflect what we want to become as an organization? After another round of layoffs, how will they even trust what we say?

How do I create a marketing strategy that business owners will own and want to implement instead of check off a list as being done and then sit it on a shelf? How do I explain complex concepts in ways that folks can understand and use?

What is a student going to do with their future? Are they making the right education and career choices? Will they be happy pursuing this path?

2. Visual conversationalists play critical roles in these conversations as the expert or leader.

As Educational Director, I am the go-to resource/source of the answers for students and staff alike.

As Vice President, I am the executive with the plan, responsible for holding the big vision and making this plan a reality.

As a Marketing Consultant, I am the expert brought in to "make things work'" in someone else's business.

3. The results of these conversations have the potential to make direct and tangible impacts on people's work and lives.

My conversations impact employee trust and relationships, leadership expectations and corporate culture, ultimately affecting the sustainability of a large organization in changing times.

My conversations influence students' future career and life choices and general quality of life.

My conversations impact budgets and returns on investment, brand and future business development and the ultimate survival and success of the venture.

4. Visual conversationalists need to create open and interactive conversations in order to support and ensure successful outcomes.

I cannot change my company's culture without engaging everyone within the company to take part in creating the new one.

I cannot help a business be successful without that business showing up and taking an active part in making success happen.

I cannot help a student plan for their future without the student's own participation and insights.

It does not matter if you are a high-level executive, a mid-level academic director helping students with life decisions, or a marketing consultant working with small businesses on an individual basis. In each case, high-stakes conversations are taking place that have the potential to directly impact the outcome of other people's personal and professional lives.

As I found out early on in my career as a Stick Figure Strategist®, even military Special Forces units fall under these four commonalities. One incoming commanding officer of a recently reunited Special Forces division had contacted me to graphically facilitate a two-day strategic visioning and teambuilding workshop. This officer was a creative, out-of-the-box leader who understood if you wanted soldiers to truly *own* their Division's history, purpose and mission, the soldiers had to co-create this shared history, purpose and mission. Hosting visual conversations, we created an environment where the soldiers could leave rank outside the room and speak freely. This process allowed them to loosen up, find their voice and truly engage in the process. Everyone who was part of the conversation knew they were being heard because everything they shared instantly became visible on the page. It was tangible proof that everything said had equal weight, regardless of the rank of the person saying the idea. By the end of our workshop, every soldier was the proud creator of a single "Commando Vision" that continues to motivate and unite them to this day.[3]

Perhaps you are a small business owner who needs to communicate and get clear on a product or service experience to ensure your business' long-term success. Or perhaps you may be a city manager who is directly responsible for getting everyone excited and on the same page about moving forward on a neighborhood project. You may even be a parent who wants to draw your kids into the conversation. Whatever the case, it is important to be able to make your participants feel heard and included and make their outcomes clear.

In today's world, as even U.S. Army Special Forces units can relate, "business as usual" is no longer getting the job done. It is time to mix it up and get people actively engaged and participating in conversations. People are inspired, learn and remember in different ways—why not leverage this?

> *"Your ability to communicate is an important tool in your pursuit of your goals, whether it is with your family, your co-workers or your clients and customers."*
> LES BROWN

What Does a Visual Conversation Look Like?

Let's start by getting to the crux of what a conversation actually is. The New Oxford English Dictionary defines "conversation" as "the informal exchange of ideas by spoken words."[4]

For our purposes, we are going to interpret "words" loosely, to include written words and icons and interpret "spoken" as drawn. I want you to be able to create a visual "conversation" after drawing your way through this book. As it turns out, drawing works pretty well for this conversational format. So, let's break it down:

"Conversation" Deconstructed

1. Informal Exchange: The informal exchange in a conversation requires give and take. It is not a one-sided presentation, persuasion or barrage. Exchange requires an interaction of some kind and being approachable is the key to informality.

Visual conversations have the unique ability to create balance AND approachability. By working on paper in a shared space, or whiteboards in the open, the setting makes it extremely easy for people to jump in and join the conversation. A visual conversation environment allows for participants to voice feedback on what has been drawn, even to pick up a marker and join in the drawing like my classmates joined me in Mrs. Schultz's class. The act of drawing simply and loosely—and drawing *together*—keeps things informal. Drawing ideas in real-time says by default, "these ideas are not perfect, they are not finished'," and therefore there is room for correction, improvement and evolution. (Plus, there is also room for others to contribute to the drawing!)

2. Of Ideas: Here, you can let ideas flow freely. They can range from a thought or suggestion to a possible course of action, a concept or mental impression of a thing, an

> *"Let us make a special effort to stop communicating with each other, so we can have some conversation."*
> MARK TWAIN

opinion or belief about something or a feeling that something is probable or possible. Anything is fair game. We are also talking about those big ideas that may seem hard to capture – the aim or purpose of a thing. It is interesting to note that the origin of "idea" came from the Greek word *idea*, meaning "form or pattern," and from the base of *idein*, meaning, "to see."[5] Ideas, from the start, were established to help us see. Through your drawings, you are going to make ideas REALLY easy to see!

3. By Spoken Words: Spoken words are simply single, distinct and meaningful elements of communication used to represent remarks or pieces of information. They are essentially auditory symbols with meanings that have been agreed upon. Similarly, a drawing or icon is a representative symbol of that same remark or piece of information. If you were able to learn to use spoken words to communicate, you can easily learn to use other symbols to communicate as well!

Different Types of Conversation[6]

We were all built to converse. In fact, try going through the day without having a conversation with anyone. Not the mailman, not the barista at your local coffeehouse...not even with yourself. It's a hard thing to do!

Although conversations can and do take place in all sorts of contexts—both formal and informal—the word "conversation" usually refers to a relaxed, casual exchange. As a visual conversationalist, you are going to encounter various types of conversations (sometimes even within the same conversation!) at one time or another. Some of the key types of conversations you will encounter are **chats**, **dialogues**, **arguments** or **parleys**, **colloquy** and **communion**.

Some of these types may sound familiar to you, while others you may only be hearing of for the first time. Don't let this daunt you! These are merely the written

words used to describe what you have most likely experienced many times over in your day-to-day life. The important part is to understand the "feel" and purpose of conversations so you can determine how to best support the conversation visually. Here is a brief run-down of the six most common types of conversations you will encounter, courtesy of my Oxford English Dictionary:[7]

A **chat** is the least formal of all conversations, consisting of talking with another in a familiar or informal manner. Whether it is a father talking to his son about girls, two women having a heart-to-heart talk about their

relationships or two co-workers talking over lunch, this conversation is generally open and relaxed.

A **dialogue** is a more specific conversation where all parties involved are expressing their (often opposing) opinions on a specific issue or topic. Dialogue can take place in any area of life: couples can get into a dialogue about whether they want to spend money on a new house, lively dialogues can spring up around religion or politics, or executive teams can get into a dialogue about the pros and cons of a new management process.

You know you've stepped into an **argument** when the participants are passionately or heatedly discussing different points of view that are clearly in opposition. Argument can also play a role in a **parley**, which is the formal way to describe a discussion between enemies regarding the terms of a truce.

A **colloquy** is the most formal of all conversations. Participants can enter into a colloquy on religious or theological matters, the state of the environment, or even nuclear disarmament (you get the picture). It can also be used to jokingly describe a guarded exchange (i.e. a brief colloquy with the arresting officer).

Lastly, we have a **communion** (and no, I am not referring to Holy Communion.) Communion is also a form of conversation that typically consists of sharing a strong (often emotional) exchange of thoughts or feelings. Sometimes communion takes place on such a profound level that no words are necessary (i.e. communion with nature).

A 'Conversational' Activity

Odds are good you are already having all these different types of conversations without even thinking about it! Having a visual conversation is simply another type of conversation, but with a visible—and visual—outcome.

What types of conversation are you most likely going to encounter as a practicing visual conversationalist? Take a few minutes to identify them and mark them in the bubbles below.

> *The real takeaway here is this: if you have had these conversations you can have visual conversations as well. And I am going to show you how!*

Remember our three people (Alli, Pops and Becks) at the start of this chapter? Let's take a look at how they could solve their challenges through visual conversations:

Alli – Vice President of Innovation

When Alli draws out ideas with her executive leadership team, they are literally on the same page as she is.

They can follow along and see how ideas and arguments are built. They can question and clarify, challenge and co-create. And at the end of the conversation, Alli knows that her leadership team has not only comprehended what she was sharing, but they are ready to make better decisions and take the next step.

Pops – Director of Student Affairs

When Pops draws out ideas with his students or his team, they can see themselves in the bigger picture, and see themselves as part of the solution being offered. Because they helped create the drawing through their conversation, everyone is now a vested owner in the outcome, ready to take it to the next level.

They feel seen and heard and are inspired to make their vision a reality.

Becks – Business Marketing Consultant

When Becks draws out ideas with her clients, they gain clarity into their own vision of what is possible and can take the most effective and focused action to achieve their goals.

Plus, when they revisit the drawing of their visual conversation, both Becks and her client re-experience the energy and excitement they felt when creating the plan together, which reinvigorates them to keep moving forward.

ACTIVITY: What Does a Visual Conversation Look Like?

Just as conversations come in different forms, visual conversations also take different forms and shapes. So let's explore what visual conversations look like. The following are two examples on the same topic of conversation.

Conversation topic: How do you know when you are in a great conversation? How do you know when you're in a conversation that sucks? What is the difference?

For each, write down:
1. What do you *see*?
2. What do you *feel*?
3. What's the *message*?

Don't worry; there is no right or wrong answer here![18] Just see what you draw forth from these images and note your observations.

Your Turn: Think about the conversations you tend to have at work, at home and in the community. What could these visual conversations also look like?

Now Draw Forth!

Your ability to engage in powerful conversations and get teams working from the same page will be your secret for success as the world becomes increasingly more complex and interconnected. Regardless of your job, the type of conversations you engage in with your team, or even what this "team" may look like, you can up your game—and the results you achieve—by picking up a pen and becoming a visual conversationalist.

Sharpening Your Visual Language Skills

As I mentioned early on in this chapter, visual conversations are the same as that second language that you learned in junior high or high school. To keep your visual language skills sharp and continually evolving, it really is as simple as this: Use it, or lose it!

The more you use your skills, the better they will become...and the more comfortable you will become using them! After all, I draw pretty much how I did in junior high school: I have just gotten really good at it over time.

"Use It or Lose It" Actions You Can Take Every Day

- **Connect to a practice community or find a buddy to help you practice your skills.**

- **Get clear on the purpose of your own conversations, why you're having them, what you hope to accomplish and what they actually accomplish.**

- **Pay attention to the meetings and other "business-as-usual" processes you engage in right now. Where are they working? Where are they not?**

- **Look for opportunities to engage in visual conversation every day. Make it fun.**

- **JUST DO IT!**

2

Overcoming the Fear of Public (Visual) Speaking

We have looked at what visual conversations are, their value and importance. At this point, you might be feeling a bit hesitant to jump up and start drawing in front of people. Don't stress: you are not alone here. As your visual conversation coach, I am here to help you bust through any blocks you might be experiencing so you can move forward.

So, why is it sometimes so hard to dive right in? For many of us, myself included, the first time we draw conversations with others can be a bit frightening and intimidating.[1] It can even feel a bit like you are speaking in public for the very first time. And in a way, you are!

Drawing out conversations with others is like "visual" public speaking. Fear of public speaking—formally known as glossophobia—is the number one fear of 74% of people in North America.[2] Now here I am asking you to move outside of your comfort zone to learn and use a new language. In public, no less. (No, this is not scary at all!)[3]

Standing up in a very visible way, making individual ideas known and reflecting the ideas of others, using a gloriously imperfect and subjective language can leave even the best of us feeling a wee bit vulnerable. It is no wonder you may be thinking: "My drawings are Good Enough for me, but are they really Good Enough for anyone else to see?[4] Will I stumble over my visual words? What happens if I can't keep up with the conversation?"

These are all valid fears...that you have the power to BUST. I know, because when I started out, I battled through these self-same fears. Facing the blank page can be scary as hell. I still have a shred of fear every time I turn to start drawing, but it lasts for a moment and quickly passes.

The "Jackass" Myth

If public (visual) speaking sparks fear in us, then let's get down to the nitty-gritty of what this fear is all about. Fear is commonly defined as a distressing emotion aroused by impending danger or pain, whether the threat is real or imagined.[5] So, if fear is the anticipation of pain, I propose that each of us should ask ourselves, "Is this pain something real or imagined? What am I really afraid of here?"

Here are the top five fears I had when I first started drawing conversations with and for others:

What if I misspell something?

What if people look at what I draw and think it's stupid?

What if I don't know how to draw what folks are talking about in front of all these people?

What if I bend over to reach the bottom of the drawing board and my pants rip and I'm left with this big hole with my panties sticking out?[6]

What if people look at what I just drew for them and think I'M stupid?

In all reality, all five of these fears really boiled down to one basic fear: "Am I going to look like a jackass?"

This is a common fear surrounding drawing out ideas and conversations with other people. After all, nobody wants to do something and look like a fool. We (okay, I) prefer to do things we are good at, so we will look like we know what we are doing. More than this, we (I) prefer to do things that are easy for us so we (I) will look like an expert in what we are doing.

As I briefly touched on before, it was not easy for me to start drawing out ideas with other people. In fact, I resisted it.

When I first started doing this sort of work, I received an invitation from a community leader to draw out ideas as part of a huge community conversation about education. I agreed, and then I panicked. Sure, I had been drawing out ideas with people I *knew*, but this was different. I was not going to be in a room full of friends, but a room full of strangers. I got scared. So I drew up a visual template to capture and shape the conversation, leaving me free to capture content in bulleted lists. It was safe and it was easy. It was not fun or particularly rewarding—because I *wanted* to draw in front of these folks—but my fear got the better of me. Afterwards, the person who extended the invitation came up to me with a twinge of sadness in his eyes. What I had done was fine, he said, but he was really hoping to have me actually *draw* the conversation so people could see what they were talking about in the moment.

I felt like a schmuck. I had let my fears about what the group would think of my work PREVENT me from hosting a powerful visual conversation. At the end of the day, I was sad, my client was sad, and my fear of looking like a jackass left me looking and feeling like one.

It was at this point I decided to really take on my fears and get to a place where I was not only comfortable, but also raring to pick up the pen and draw out ideas with people in the moment. The next time I was asked to host a visual conversation, I took a deep breath and drew my little heart out. It was such an amazing experience, I haven't looked back since!

After my "jackass" experience, conquering my fear of public "visual speaking" ended up being surprisingly easy to accomplish. I believe this can be the case for you as well. How did I do it? That is what the rest of this chapter is about!

Milarepa Faces His Demons[7]

We are often afraid of the things we don't understand. The Buddhist story of Milarepa is a great allegory for how to overcome your fears and make friends with your inner critic.

According to Buddhist legend, a monk named Milarepa lived thousands of years ago. As wise monks tended to do back then, Milarepa lived in a cave where he meditated, studied the dharma and led an otherwise peaceful life.

One day after gathering firewood, he returned to his cave to discover that it had been overrun by demons. Crazy eyed, horned, big fanged, drooling ol' demons. They were all OVER his cave!

His first thought upon seeing them was, "I have got to get rid of them!" Grabbing a broom, he started rushing about his cave, waving his broom about and yelling, "Shoo! Shoo!"

But the demons were completely unfazed. In fact, the more he chased them, the more comfortable, settled-in and downright amused they seemed to be.

Next Milarepa thought, "Well, I am supposed to be a Buddhist. I know, I will teach these demons the dharma and they will become so enlightened they will *have* to go away!" So he struck a meditation pose and began to recite the wisdom of the great Buddhist teachings.

The demons simply sat looking back at him, as if they were patting him on the head and saying, "Oh honey, that's so cute!"

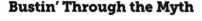

Well, this really got Milarepa's goat! And he lost it. He got good and mad and started hollering and screaming at those demons to GET OUT!

Again, the demons did not budge.

Finally, Milarepa looked at all of the demons in his cave. He took a deep breath, turned to them and said, "Well, it looks like you have come to stay. If you are going to be here, then let me make you feel at home. Come in, my friends! Please sit and rest for a while. I am open to whatever you have to teach me. May I offer you some refreshment? I have some very good Oolong tea you might enjoy. . .."

POOF!

All of the demons instantly disappeared, except for one: the biggest, most saucer-eyed, fangiest one of them all. He was still there, staring at Milarepa with those big ol' eyes.

Milarepa looked at the demon, sighed and gave up.

"Demon, I have tried everything. I have tried forcing you out. I have tried yelling you out. I have tried teaching you the dharma and I have even tried welcoming you into my home. I know there is nothing I can do against you. I also know you are not going anywhere. I give up. Eat me if you wish."

Completely letting go of any resistance or expectations, Milarepa laid his head inside the demon's mouth.

POOF!

Just like that, the demon was gone.

Bustin' Through the Myth

Busting through myths is no easy task. The only way that works for me is to consciously take steps to overcome my fears. To help you overcome your fears, I have created a mini "visual public speaking" myth-busting program. Working through the following two steps will have you visually speaking from the front of the room in no time!

Two Steps to Busting Through Your Fears:
1. Identify the Root of Your Fear
2. Cultivate a Fearless (Good Enough) Mindset

STEP ONE: Identify the Root of Your Fear
The first step for overcoming any fear of drawing out ideas in public (even with your own friends) is to be aware of and clearly identify where your fear is really coming from. The fear of looking like a jackass when drawing out ideas with others can take on many forms. These forms fall into four basic categories:

1. **Visual Language**
2. **Skill Building**
3. **Belief**
4. **Environment/External Factors**

1. Visual Language

This fear arises when we simply do not feel fluent enough in our visual language skills to communicate well with others. See if any of these sound familiar to you:

"I don't know the language well enough to communicate with ANYONE at this point!"

"I don't have a big enough visual vocabulary yet, so I can't communicate my ideas very well."

"I have no idea what to even draw!"

"How in the world do I even go about putting things in the right order?"

"I don't know how to communicate abstract ideas!"

"Nobody will even know what I was drawing!"

2. Skill Building

This fear arises when we feel our skills are not strong enough to use with others. This fear makes negative self-talk like the following statements surface:

"What if I run out of paper before the conversation is done?"

"I can't draw."

"There is no way I can draw fast enough. I would just slow down the conversation while folks wait for me to finish drawing."

"My handwriting is terrible and I am a bad speller!"

"How am I supposed to draw, talk AND listen all at the same time?"

D'OH!

3. Belief

This one convinces us we do not have the necessary abilities to be a successful visual conversationalist. In this scenario, we limit ourselves to our comfort zone and often hold the following limiting beliefs:

"It is not going to turn out the way I wish it would. It is going to be all messy!"

"I will feel so self-conscious standing up there drawing."

"I can't do this, I am [fill in the blank]!"

"How can my drawings possibly help someone else? I can barely draw a stick figure!"

"Someone is going to criticize me. I am going to get it wrong!"

4. Environment/External Factors

These can also play a strong part in what fears manifest inside us. In this situation, we do not think our environment will tolerate us drawing out ideas with others, and the following negative self-talk can surface:

"You may be able to do that at other places, but it would never fly here!"

"Folks won't take it seriously."

"My team is too serious... they would never go for it."

"Sure, they *say* they want us to be creative...but they don't really mean it."

"It is not professional!"

"Don't try to win over the haters; you are not a jackass whisperer."
BRENÉ BROWN

As you went through these four root causes of fear did you happen to notice they all had something in common? The vast majority of these speak to a fear or concern of being able to do a thing *Good Enough*.

So our fear of looking like a jackass really boils down to: **"Will I be able to do this stuff Good Enough?"**

Want the short answer? Here it is:

You CAN draw Good Enough. The key is to let yourself feel your fear and do it anyway![8] In feeling your fear, you become aware of what it is. You become able to identify the root cause and name it. This, my friend, is half the battle!

STEP TWO: Cultivate a Fearless (Good Enough) Mindset

The second half of the battle for overcoming your fears—once and for all—is cultivating a fearless (Good Enough) mindset. In the remainder of this section we will unpack how key aspects of a Good Enough mindset can help you overcome any fears keeping you from picking up the pen and drawing out ideas with your team.

What you draw is Good Enough to get your ideas across!

Remember:

What you drew—or did not draw—as a kid does NOT define you as a visual conversationalist. If you recall, I was the "tracer" in the family, tracing over images while my mother and sister drew beautiful freehand drawings. I did not pick up a pen and really start drawing out ideas until I was in my 30s![9]

You don't have to have graphic artist skills or an art school background to draw out ideas. My career was in nonprofit management before starting my business as a Stick Figure Strategist®. I have friends with backgrounds in biotech, education, sales, and landscape maintenance that draw out ideas. So your current work or career path does not matter—this visual language stuff translates across any field or industry. You can draw out ideas in a Good Enough way regardless of who you are, what you do or where you work!

It is totally normal to want to draw better than you already do. Do not let this stop you! I would LOVE to be able to draw better than I currently do! I daydream about being able to draw comic books and cartoons with ease.

I have scores of sketchbooks filled with different figures and expressions to build my skills. However, I am also in a sweet spot of liking what I draw AND seeing opportunities to improve. Rest assured, even the "Pros" wish they could draw better, but it does not stop us from picking up the pen. What you and I have in common is the ability to draw ideas Good Enough to get our points across and facilitate visual conversations. *This* is where I want you to land.

Your Good Enough drawing skills are good enough for now. More power to you for evolving these skills over time! Just don't let fears of creating "not Good Enough" drawings prevent you from picking up a chalk, pen or marker and drawing. Start playing and having fun with this stuff now!

The Head Game: Cultivating Mindset

What this really all comes down to is: Your ability to draw Good Enough is all in your head. So let's work on the head game!

In my experience, there are four key steps to cultivating a winning head game as a visual conversationalist:

1. **Befriend Your Inner Critic**

2. **Give Yourself Permission**

3. **Take Imperfect Action**

4. **Be Good Enough**

STEP 1. Befriend Your Inner Critic

Have you ever heard a quiet voice whispering in your ear that what you do is not good enough? That you are inadequate for the task? Not worthy of picking up the pen? If so, you are not alone! (I have been there with you for sure!)

This critical voice you hear inside your head is called the "Inner Critic." It is a concept used in popular psychology to refer to a sub-personality everyone has in some form.[10] As you may have experienced before now, your inner critic's job it is to judge you, demean you and otherwise undermine your self-confidence. (Great! Thanks, popular psychology!)

Inner Critics Come in All Shapes and Sizes

Your inner critic can take many forms.[11] As you get to know your inner critic, you will discover it has several different facets and personas that show up in different ways. Over the years, I have paid close attention to how my inner critic shows up for me. So far, I have had the pleasure to meet twelve—yes, twelve!—different aspects of my inner critic! Let me introduce you to them:

The Bully

I'll sock you one!"

The Comparison Queen

"Who's the fairest? Not you!"

The Perfectionist

White Glove

"Is it REALLY good enough?"

The Silent Martyr

"I'll just suffer and the world will thank me one day."

The Dream Stealer

"Go ahead. Get your hopes up. Too bad you can't really do it."

The Doom & Gloomer

"Not only is the glass half-empty, but I've dumped it out on the floor just to show you!"

The Partying Cheerleader

Hey, it's okay! Woo Hoo! Do what you want, it doesn't matter!"

The Guru

"Your body doesn't matter... live outside of your body, because only your spirit really matters."

The Good Girl

"I'm trying REALLY hard to please you"

The Loveless

"Don't come looking to me for anything, I've got nothing for you!"

The Rational Robot

If Then

"The logical thing to do would be this, but you are illogical . . . illogical!"

The Shoe Chucker

"I'm tired of waiting for that other shoe to drop, so let's chuck it at your head!"

Now let's get to know your inner critic and all its facets!

ACTIVITY: Draw Your Inner Critic(s)

Read through the previous inner critic descriptions. Which ones do you recognize in yourself? Are any aspects or forms missing from this list? Feel free to give them a name and add them!

Think about each and every facet of your inner critics. Visualize them in your mind. Now draw a Good Enough picture of them to focus on. We will use these drawings in the next activity.

Befriending Your Inner Critic

Now that you have gotten to know the various forms of your inner critics a wee bit, there are essentially three things you can choose to do:

1. Let your Inner Critic continue to behave in your head as it always has. . . and do nothing.

2. Try to kick it out of your head and get rid of it once and for all.

3. Learn how to make friends with your inner critic and transform it into your ally.

At this point, you may have guessed I am a huge advocate of making friends. Here is why:

When I first paid attention to my inner critic, I wanted every aspect of it out of my head for good! And I tried, just like our Buddhist monk friend, Milarepa, to get it out. But the more I tried to drive it out, meditate it out, ignore it, or insult it away, the stronger and more at home my inner critic became. It was not until I finally gave up the notion of getting rid of my inner critic, and instead dedicated myself to befriending it, that its effects and influences changed. I cannot say that life is always sunshine and smiles, because—just like with any friendship—we have our good days and bad days. But in general, we have learned how to work better together. . . and this has made all the difference!

5 Steps to Befriending Your Inner Critic

Remember Milarepa and his demons? Every aspect of your inner critic likes to take residence in your head, the same way those demons liked to take residence in Milarepa's cave. While each inner critic can have negative aspects, our inner critics are actually somewhat misguided attempts at helping us become our best selves.[12] Fortunately, you don't have to be eaten by demons to make friends with your inner critic! Here are the basic steps to turning your inner critic into your friend:

1. Recognize when your inner critic is present.
2. Feel the discomfort when it shows up.
3. Realize it has something else to share with you, above and beyond making you feel uncomfortable.
4. Ask for the deeper lesson and listen to what your inner critic has to say.
5. Trust that your inner critic is not there to eat you, and appreciate how it can help you grow and evolve.

Birth of an Inner Critic

When I was in the fifth grade, I was a fast and prolific writer. Unfortunately, being a fast writer did not translate into being a careful speller. Even when copying words, I would misspell them because I was just doing things so quickly. So of course, it was only natural that my dad got me a misspeller's dictionary as a Christmas present that year.

You can understand why I was surprised when, the next Christmas, my dad gave me another misspeller's dictionary as a gift.

So I said, "Gee, thanks Dad, but you already gave me one of these last year for Christmas."

To which he said, in a voice dripping with sarcasm, "Really? Are you sure about that? Because you don't seem to actually use it."[13] (Ouch!) Guess whose voice my inner critic occasionally adopts?

ACTIVITY: Make Friends With Your Inner Critic

Start by revisiting what you wrote and drew in the previous activity. For each aspect of your Inner Critic you identified do the following:

1. Which aspects show up more often than others? Which are occasional visitors?

_____
_____
_____

2. Note when these facets of your inner critic tend to show up in your head. Who are you with? What are you doing? Where are you? When are they most likely to pop up? What do they tend to say when they show up? What do you notice about why they are there?

_____
_____
_____
_____

3. Notice if any of your inner critic's voices sound familiar to you. If they do, this is okay. (There are times when my inner critic sounds a lot like my Dad!)

_____
_____

4. What gift is your inner critic trying to give to you, even if not in a graceful or particularly effective way? How does it want to help you grow and evolve?

_____
_____
_____
_____

Now draw what you discovered about your inner critic in the space below.

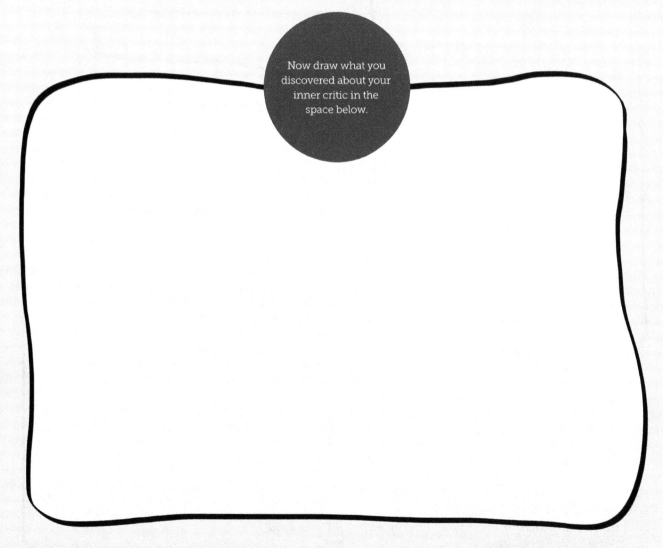

ACTIVITY: For Stubborn Critics, Try the Chair

Now that you have gotten to know your inner critics a bit better, take a moment and draw the most amazing chair you can think of for them. It is comfy, it is gorgeous and it is just for your inner critic. Okay, do you have your inner critic's chair in mind? Sketch it out in the space below.

Now, any time you need to work without your inner critic interrupting your process or butting in, have it hang out in its special chair. Let it know that when you need input you will come over and ask for their help. When you are done with what you are working on, you will come back and retrieve them. But for right now, this is your inner critic's opportunity to enjoy some "me time" in this most special of spots! (My inner critic likes to hang out in a cushy armchair at the coffee house. Where is your chair located?)

STEP 2. *Give Yourself Permission*

Once you have befriended your inner critic, you may notice that it is easier to give yourself permission to pick up the pen and draw out ideas with people. If you have not already done so, give yourself permission to do the following:

- **Pick up the pen and draw something with people.**

- **Play with drawing out ideas and enjoy the process.**

- **Bring more creativity, enjoyment and expression to your work.**

- **Draw the absolutely worst looking stick people in the world and STILL have it be Good Enough to get your ideas across.**

- **Be imperfect and vulnerable in front of ANYONE... including yourself!**

What do you need to give yourself permission to do? Stop waiting and sign off on a permission slip!

ACTIVITY: Write Out a Permission Slip

Create your own or download a template from my website at jeannelking.com/drawforth/resources. Make sure to sign it from the person who most needs to give you permission to play with drawing and drawing out ideas. Is this you? Your inner critic? Someone else?

If you are not sure who needs to sign your permission slip, journal about it to discover whose voice you hear when you feel your stuff is "not Good Enough". What are they saying? What do they mean to say, but are not saying particularly well? What do you most need to hear from this voice? What does this voice most need to hear from you?

STEP 3. Take Imperfect Action

As a visual conversationalist, I hear some variation of this statement from participants every time I do a project: "I wish I could draw, but I can't because [fill in the blank with a disparaging remark or two.]"

Well guess what. You can draw. . . and what you draw is Good Enough to get your ideas across! Simply allow yourself to take *imperfect action*. You could do it when you were five years old, and you can do it now!

Taking imperfect action is all about non-judgment. Sometimes what holds us back from doodling or drawing in public is the notion, "I can't draw" or "my drawings look stupid." We fall into the trap of wanting what we create to look absolutely perfect—or at least close to what we envisioned in our heads! Sometimes, this desire for perfection can ultimately keep us from taking any action at all. We prepare, we think about it, we wish we could . . . but we never actually "do." It is a "ready, aim, fire" approach, only we "ready, aim, aim, aim, aim" and never actually fire!

Imperfect action means to, as Nike coined, "Just Do It." It is not going to be perfect. It may not even be amazingly gorgeous. You may need to add arrows pointing to something you drew, just to identify what it is because it is such a hot mess of a drawing. This is GREAT! Doing things imperfectly means you are *doing* them, and this is going to allow you to do them better in the future. This "firing" provides feedback, helping you to get ready and aim better for next time.

One way to practice imperfect action is to doodle your thoughts in a visual journal that nobody sees but you. In this journal, practice expressing yourself in words and pictures. For the words and ideas that mean something special to you, start creating your own visual vocabulary and use these icons consistently to create a visual grammar you are used to. Remember: this is a visual journal just for you, so it does not matter what it looks like. . . especially to your inner critic, who may be tempted to point out all the ways your work does not stand up to Picasso's. Mine certainly wants to! I will let you in on a little secret: when my inner critic starts to get all negative and critical like that, I simply send her to Starschmucks and her special chair

with full permission for her to do whatever she wants there, then I keep on drawing with a smile on my face. (Good thing I have an unlimited supply of Starschmucks gift cards with no expiration date!)

Imperfect action beats perfect inaction any day!

STEP 4. Be Good Enough

Rest assured, everything you need to establish a Good Enough mindset already lies within you. The two most powerful inner tools you possess are persistence and confidence—you may just need to exercise and strengthen their muscle memory a bit.

Persistence is what keeps you drawing, even when your inner critic is doing its darndest to get you to put down the pen (or stylus or stick at the beach) to go do something—ANYTHING—else. Well guess what? The more you draw, the more comfortable you will get with drawing! (Not to mention how much better you will get at it!) Remember: my style is pretty much the same as it was in junior high school—I have just gotten better over time at drawing this way!

Confidence is also key to drawing Good Enough. When you draw, you reveal a part of yourself not many others may have been privy to before. As you share your thoughts and ideas in visual form, people may not always like or agree with what you express. Therefore, to BE Good Enough you have to be willing to take a risk. After all, it is one thing to draw in your journal in the privacy of your own home; it is another thing to do something "imperfectly" in front of other people—especially people you respect and want to impress.

Of all your tools, confidence is the most important. You have to believe in what you draw, because in order to draw Good Enough, you have to believe that YOU are good enough!

Now Draw Forth!

It is normal to feel some fear about drawing out ideas with other people, especially when you are just starting to do this. It is a new activity, you are still building skills and experience, and it is also an incredibly vulnerable action to take because you are willingly taking an imperfect action in front of others. This takes guts. Guts, quite frankly, that not many people display nowadays.

We are all perfectly content to do what comes easy to us. To do the safe things we know are "okay." That won't stretch our limits or put us in a position of taking any sort of risk.

I *really* get this. After all, I never wanted to own my own business.

Actually, let me rephrase that. Prior to 2010, had anyone asked me if I wanted to own my own business, my answer would have been an immediate and automatic "HELLS no!" followed by a hand clapping over my mouth and apologetic look on my face for actually saying that thought out loud.

Now that I am a business owner, though, I cannot imagine doing anything else! Starting my own business ended up being one of the best, most rewarding, exciting and empowering things I ever could have done for myself. Perhaps drawing out conversations in real time with your team can be this for you.

So please don't let fear or doubt or uncertainty keep you from drawing out ideas. Choose to get your head in the game, pick up the pen and draw forth the best in your family, community or team! Because what you draw, what you do, and who you ARE is Good Enough!

10 Tips for an Awesome "Good Enough" Mindset

1. There is no one "right" way to draw a conversation. Whatever you do is exactly what needs to happen for that particular conversation.

2. Keep your sense of humor!

3. Keep an open mind and enjoy the process.

4. Your work does not have to be pretty; your work has to be accessible, legible, understandable, even inviting to participants. Stick figures can work for this!

5. Have faith in your abilities: what you draw is Good Enough!

6. WHO you are is Good Enough! (Dammit!)

7. Don't be afraid to push yourself outside your boundaries.

8. Give yourself permission to play!

9. Send your inner critic to Starschmucks or their comfy chair!

10. Have fun!

PART 2:
Tools & Language

3

Your Toolkit

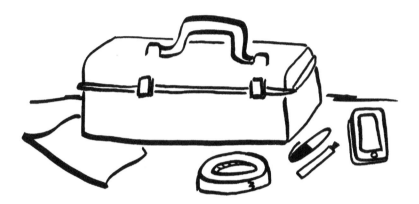

One of the greatest things about being a visual conversationalist is it does not take much to get started. Although there are some basic tools you will want or need to buy, many of the tools are already at your disposal. The reason I say this is because being a successful visual conversationalist requires having a toolkit that consists of both *external* and *internal* tools.

External Tools: What You Have at the "Drawing Board"

Your external toolkit will consist of all the physical tools and materials you will need at the "drawing board" to actually draw out conversations. These basic supplies are simple to access and relatively cheap to purchase. In theory, you can draw conversations using the everyday office supplies you have lying about your workspace. When engaged in an important visual conversation, however, you don't want low quality supplies working against you. (Few things are worse than drawing a conversation on a big piece of paper taped to the wall... only to discover as you take down the sheet that your markers bled through the paper and left a lovely pattern behind. Oops!)

To give you a leg-up, I am going to share my "essential" list of tried-and-true tools you will find useful as a visual conversationalist, along with where I like to get my supplies for visual conversations.

Two Types of External Tools

When it comes to visual conversations, you really only need two external tools: something to draw *on* and something to draw *with*. These can be a piece of paper and a marker, a smartphone and your finger, or—if you are on a desert island—it could even be a sandy beach and a stick!

We will talk more about the implications associated with your choice of materials in just a moment. For now, let's explore some of the tools available to you to "draw on" and "draw with."

"Draw On" - Surfaces for Drawing Forth Visual Conversations

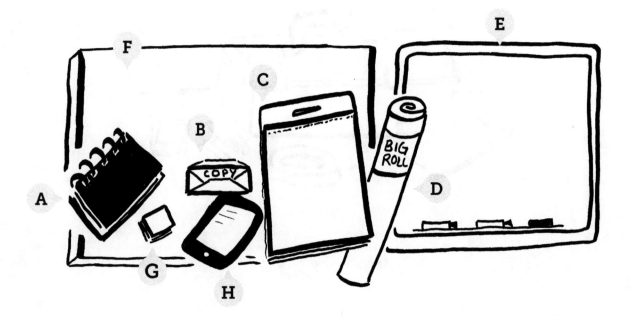

Sketchbook (A)

Any kind of sketchbook is fine—a fancy hardcover journal or a cheap sketchpad will work. Pick one you will feel comfortable drawing in and taking with you wherever you go. Also play with the size of the sketchbook and how it opens. I personally use a variety of sizes: I use pocket-sized sketchbooks to capture one idea per page, and larger (9"x12" and up) sketchbooks to capture the flow of ideas. I like to work landscape on the page (where the page is wider than it is tall), so I tend to look for a sketchbook with a spiral binding so it will lay flat on the short side of the book like a stenographer's pad.

Copy Paper (B)

Copy paper is great for doodling and drawing out ideas you won't need to preserve long-term. Buy a ream of inexpensive letter-size paper and keep it handy for drawing out ideas.

Draw Forth Tip: I recycle my copy paper drawings by using the other side as printer paper for internal jobs.

Flip Chart Paper (C)

Perfect for small groups, flip chart paper is large enough for folks to see and interact with, yet small enough to be used in practically any workspace.

Roll Paper (D)

If you are working with larger groups or bigger problem sets, it helps to increase the size and scale of your work. My current favorite roll paper is #30 sign writer's bond, which I can cut to size to fit the wall space I want to use.

Whiteboards (E)

Whether they are room-sized or personal-sized, whiteboards are an excellent reusable surface for drawing out ideas.

Hint: Be sure to snap a photo or two to preserve the conversation before you have to erase it! If you don't need it, you can always delete the photo but few things are worse than erasing something and having someone say, "WAIT! We should have kept that!"

Draw Forth Tip: The best way to erase permanent marker from a whiteboard is to scribble over it with a dry erase marker. This works nine times out of ten![1]

Paper Boards (Foam core, cardboard, etc.) (F)

Paper boards are perfect for visual conversations that need to literally stand on their own. The extra heft of these surfaces allows you to construct freestanding shapes you can draw on.

Sticky Notes (G)

I should own stock in 3M, I love sticky notes so much! These are great for doing a brain dump of ideas or information because they allow you to organize it in innumerable ways—rearranging, clustering and sorting to make new connections and meaning. I use paper sticky notes AND static cling ones. My favorite static ones are Stattys from Germany.[2] They stick to pretty much anything, come in a variety of sizes and colors and you can use a permanent marker on one side and a dry-erase marker on the white side so you can reuse and recycle them as well.

Digital Surfaces (H)

Thanks to ever-developing technology, digital surface options are rapidly growing. At the time of this writing, smartphones, tablet laptops, mini tablets, digital drawing tablets that connect to your computer and even SMART Boards® can be found in schools, workplaces, boardrooms, and—I would even venture to guess—your home.

I started off using a lower-end digital drawing tablet hooked up to my computer, but found it was a bit like drawing in a mirror. It was awkward for me to use because it did not allow me to see what or where I was drawing. I eventually transitioned to an iPad, which has become my number one digital drawing tool. I use Sketchbook® Pro to draw on because its "layers" functionality is a girl's best friend![3] When I am just sketching out a quick idea, I turn to Paper (another app). Should I need to record a drawing process for any reason, I turn to an older copy of the Brushes app that retains the "record" functionality.

This is a good time to take a moment and talk about the implications of your choice of medium when considering what you are going to use to draw forth visual conversations.

Which Medium is Right for Me?

Different mediums have very real implications for the type of visual conversation you are going to have, as well as how your conversation will unfold.

When it Comes to the Medium You Choose, Size Matters

1. Paper and Pens: The pros to using pen and paper are they don't crash, they are relatively easy to share and use with others, they have good longevity and can be translated into easily-sharable formats (such as digital images). Paper comes in a variety of sizes, from sticky notes to poster-sized and beyond. Because of this, you can choose the size of paper that is most readily visible and accessible for your group and work accordingly.

2. Whiteboard and Markers: Whiteboards and markers don't crash either—although they do dry out or fade—and they are sometimes easier to see than sketchbook-sized paper when working with small groups (although the brightness and "juiciness" of the markers can affect visibility as well). However, unless you have one of those SMART Boards® and know how to use it, your work won't necessarily last long. Odds are good if you run out of space and need to keep going, you will have to erase what you have done and then lose in-room access to this prior thinking. You may have captured an image of it on your smartphone, but it is a bit hard to process all this good information from such a tiny image. And unless you have

a rolling whiteboard or are using portable whiteboards or whiteboard sheets, your visual conversation will be held where the whiteboard is (not always the best thing).

3. Digital Surface: You can use your tablet, laptop, or another digital tool to draw out ideas during your visual conversations. On the upside, the image can immediately be saved to a digital file, making it easy to share. With the right set of skills it can be almost as easy as drawing on paper. Several colleagues of mine truly love working on their tablets this way. On the downside, one person typically creates tablet work. This means only one person can really interact with the drawing at any given time: the holder of the tablet or stylus. The other two formats encourage and allow for natural collaboration and co-drawing. One work-around is to project the tablet's work surface so others in the room can see what is happening and share their insights and feedback with the person with the tablet, but they cannot easily or directly contribute to the piece. In my book, this does not make for a great conversation—only a great presentation. Not to mention, software can crash and batteries can drain.

Other mediums will continue to present themselves and break new ground, but we are going to discuss these three main choices and focus on the ones that are more tangible and easier to share amongst your team.

At-A-Glance Guide

Size	Medium	Pro	Con	Best for:
Small	Paper (e.g. sketchbook)	Intimate, easy to share with one, easy to scan and share, easy to photograph	Harder to share with group, hard to see with group in real time	Self, 1:1 sharing
Small	Whiteboard (e.g. personal whiteboard)	Easy to carry	Limited surface space requires frequent erasure	Self, drafting or sketch workspace not requiring saving
Small	Tablet (e.g. iPad)	Easy to carry, easy to use when skill is developed, easy to share electronically	Hard to draw with group, hard to see with group without projection/hook-up	Self, online
Medium	Paper (e.g. flip chart)	Easy to share with smaller group, portable, easy to photograph	Harder to scan and share, requires different skills for legible writing, etc., requires easel or wall/door space	Personal planning, small group planning
Medium	Whiteboard (e.g. small office whiteboard)	Easy to see, easy to erase	Harder to transport, glare and ink coverage create challenges in photographing	Personal, small office meetings
Medium	Digital (e.g. SMART® Board)	Visible size, easy to see, built-in saving mechanism	Learning curve	Tech savvy people and groups, drawing over presentations or other documents on display
Large	Paper (e.g. roll poster paper, recording walls, etc.)	Easy to see with a larger group, technology does not crash, permanence, can easily interact with content	Needs projection to be seen by larger groups, requires space	Big ideas, big groups, ideas you want to preserve, conferences, presentations, pitches, interactive sessions
Large	Whiteboard (e.g. conference room whiteboard, whiteboard walls)	Flexible surface for drawing out impermanent conversation records, can easily interact with content	Impermanent, inks can be hard to see, glare, challenge to photograph, saving what is on it precludes use of board again	Exploratory sessions, brainstorming, idea generation
Large	Digital (e.g. tablet and projection)	Visible as large as your projection surface is, easily saved, easily shared electronically	Others cannot easily add to the drawing	Conferences, all-hands meetings

A Happy Medium

There is no one "right" medium to use. Rather, it depends on your personal preferences. Many of the people I know use paper to draw out their ideas, but the size of paper can range from small sketchbooks to giant wall-sized posters or murals. Plus, many of us use different mediums for different types of conversations or projects. I use small sketchbooks for personal ideas and notes, whiteboards and sticky notes for brainstorming and brain-dumping sessions, flip charts for small group conversations and coaching sessions, large paper for larger group conversations and digital tablets for my illustration work.

The important thing is to match your choice of medium to the purpose of your work. Having an intimate conversation? Go small. Working with a big group or an important conversation? Go big! Capturing your own personal notes? Use what you like. Need quick or easy electronic sharing? Go digital. Going through iterations of ideas and don't need to hold on to those ideas very tightly? Use a whiteboard.

Working Small

Some visual conversationalists like to limit their work to the size of a Moleskine® sketchbook two-page spread. Other folks—myself included—like to use small sketchbooks to capture one idea per page during a conversation. It is like creating a series of insight flash cards. Still others like using the comic book or storyboard approach of working within a series of small panels or frames to draw forth the story within the conversation.

> *"I'm a great believer that any tool that enhances communication has profound effects in terms of how people can learn from each other, and how they can achieve the kind of freedoms that they're interested in."*
>
> BILL GATES

"Draw With" — Implements for Actually Drawing These Conversations

Markers (I)

Large markers are the visual conversationalist's tools of choice. Big fat lines force you to stay large and big in your concepts. On the other hand, pens produce finer lines, making you run the risk of your ideas getting lost in the details.

I always recommend using water-based, nontoxic markers, because they give off less fumes than permanent markers. This may not seem like a big deal until you are in a small space drawing with these fumes for several hours. Let me tell you: you want markers with the lowest fumes you can find!

Dry Erase Markers (J)

The variety of dry erase markers has exploded in recent years. These days you can get them in a rainbow of colors AND a variety of sizes! My favorites are made by Neuland® and come as chisel point markers, brush markers and jumbo tip chisel markers for big bold headers and lines. As an added bonus, they are also refillable.

Draw Forth Tip: If you are only going to go for two colors for your whiteboard work, try using high-contrast black and red. If you are going to use a rainbow palette of dry erase markers, remember that the colors you choose have meaning. (More about this in chapter 7.)

Pastels (K)

Adding color and depth to your conversations is a good way to keep people engaged in the drawing while digesting content, as well as a great way to visually organize and emphasize information. I started off using chalk pastels in stick form because this is what I was familiar with at the time. However, since the emergence of PanPastel® artist's pastels—chalk pastels that are in circular "compacts" and are applied with a wide variety of tools—they are ALL I use! These are my personal favorite for adding color accents and bold swathes of color in a hurry.

Pens (L)

I don't recommend fine point pens for visual conversations unless the conversation is just between you and another person and you are drawing on a small surface (small notebook, copy paper, back of a napkin, et cetera). Otherwise, it is too tempting to bog yourself down in the details of an idea before its time. For bigger ideas, use bigger markers!

Pencils (M)

Pencils are a bit on the light side for larger group conversations. Plus their thin point makes it tempting to follow a rabbit hole of detail. The advantage is you can erase your marks!

Draw Forth Tip: Don't want to have to spend time erasing pencil marks from your visual conversation's drawing? Try using a blue non-photo pencil instead of a regular graphite one. It is specially designed so as not to show up in photographs.

Crayons (N)

These are a great way to unleash your inner five-year-old's creativity during a meeting. Crayons come in a wide variety of colors, have a scent that evokes the creativity and play of childhood, and they won't mess your fingers the way markers can. (Although, depending on your childhood, they may be tempting to chew on!)

Paint Markers (O)

These are especially good for drawing on dark surfaces. Light colored options are high contrast and visible against dark backgrounds. Beware of those fumes, though, and make sure you are working in a large, well-ventilated place!

Stylus (P)

Using a stylus will get you the closest to recapturing the experience of drawing with pen and paper, while still allowing you to work on a digital surface. Some folks like the precision a hard-tipped stylus brings to the table, while others like the soft "smooshy" rubber stylus tips.

Finger (Q)

The late Steve Jobs' personal choice for a stylus was his finger.[4] And why not? It is always with us, hard to lose and ready at a moment's notice. Thanks to many digital platforms' abilities to zoom into a drawing, the large tip of your finger is no longer a barrier to seeing what you are drawing. The finger is my favorite stylus, too! (Particularly because there is no smooshy rubber tip to come off at inconvenient moments! I cannot tell you how many styluses I have gone through because the rubber drawing tip has simply ripped off.)

Other Handy Tools

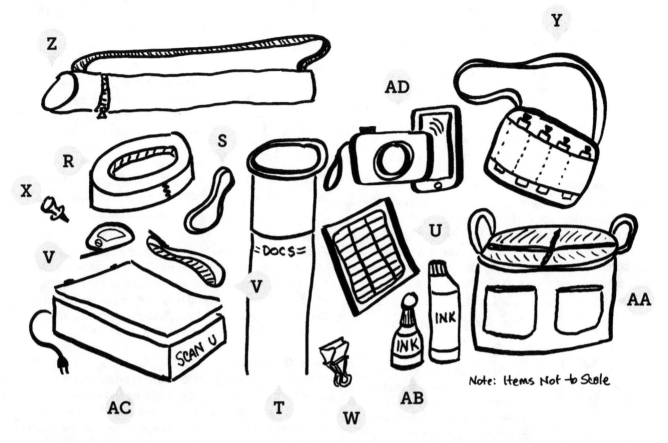

Note: Items Not to Scale

Artist Tape (R)
Artist tape has a low-tack adhesive and when used carefully it can be removed from paper and walls without damaging the surface. (Your friends and clients will thank you!)

Rubber Bands (S)
Rubber bands are great for securing rolls of paper without damaging them.

Document Tubes (T)
Use document tubes to protect your drawings and other visual conversation artifacts, such as flip chart pages or table drawings.

White Address Labels (U)
When you make a mistake on the computer you can just hit the "undo" key and it is gone. Alternatively, when you make a mistake on paper you can use a white address label to "white out" any marks you would rather not keep. I always keep a variety of sizes on-hand in my tool kit: return address labels, address labels, shipping labels, half-sheet and full page.

Draw Forth Tip: If you get address labels with the silver backing, you won't see the old mark through the label. These are also great to use for labeling your larger conversation drawings that might be stored in a document tube!

Paper Cutter (V)
After trying scores of paper cutters, I found that I love using a wrapping paper cutter! It is cheap and does the job with much more efficiency than any of the other blades or "pro" tools I have used over the years. They are particularly great for cutting sheets of roll paper.

Draw Forth Tip: Be sure to spread the edge of the paper out with your fingers, and then put the wrapping paper cutter in the middle to give it a solid "bite" to start cutting. Without the flat tension on either side, you may have a hard time getting the paper cutter started.

A Look Inside Jeannel's Kit!

Every visual conversationalist has their own toolkit for drawing forth conversations. Mine keeps me prepared to host visual conversations at a moment's notice and on variety of scales and surface mediums. Here is what is typically in my tool kit:

- Züca® bag - for storing, organizing, and transporting my tools
- Pen basket
- Big markers
- Regular markers
- Fine markers
- Ink refills
- Paper cutters
- Artist tape
- Binder clips
- Push pins
- Dry erase markers and erasers in a variety of sizes and colors
- Sticky notes and Stattys in a variety of sizes and colors
- Pen slings (2) - because a gal's gotta have her gear!
- Portable whiteboards (cling plastic in carrying tube)...just in case!
- Roll paper and carrying case
- Folder with white address labels (assorted)
- Project documents
- Personal necessities (mints, mascara, pain killers and snacks)

Before I show up, I make sure I am rested, fed, watered, "pottied," and in comfortable, professional clothes that allow me to move about freely. I arrive unstressed by planning for plenty of travel time. Most importantly, I don't over-prepare. I do this by arriving ready to hear and see what is going on in the room, versus preparing for what I think is going to occur in the room. (There is a big difference!)

Binder Clips (W)

Binder clips are especially handy for securing paper on boards or keeping flip chart paper out of the way. Be sure to match the size of the binder clip to the width of the board you are using. Otherwise, it may cause unintended barriers to your drawing flow if you are working close to the edge of your page. I am partial to the silver ones because they blend into your paper quite nicely!

Push Pins (X)

If you are working on fabric walls, bulletin boards, or even on an old wall, using pushpins is a quick and easy way to tack paper up. Long pins are most useful for fabric walls. Always make sure it is okay to use pushpins where you are working, though, as they will leave holes behind when you remove them!

Draw Forth Tip: Use a bit of tape or one of your white address labels on the paper as a reinforcement where you will insert the pin to prevent or minimize paper rips.

Pen slings (Y)

When I put my pen slings on, folks know I am serious about the visual conversation! Pen slings hold a small collection of pens right by my side, so they are ready to access wherever I am in the room. These are great tools to use if you are working in a large space, or if you just like to know where your go-to markers are during visual conversations. I use them when working on flip charts and larger-sized conversation documents.

Paper Carrying Case (Z)

Carrying cases make transporting paper a breeze while minimizing any risk of damaging it. I have durable fabric cases for unused paper, and I bring document tubes with me to store and protect the finished products.

Pen Basket or Caddy (AA)

As your collection grows, I suggest organizing your markers for easy access. There are multitudes of ways to store and organize your pen collection, from shoeboxes to old greeting card display wheels! I use two old scrapbooking supply baskets for my pens. I have a large one for my entire pen and marker collection, organized by color. This one stays in my studio. When I am ready to go off and join other people for a visual conversation, I load up a smaller pen basket and pop it into my kit.

Ink Refills (AB)

Some marker collections, like Neuland® and Copic®, offer refillable options. When your marker starts getting dry from using it so much, instead of tossing it out you can simply refill the ink in your marker and keep on going! It is a much more economical way to work and reduces waste in the environment as well.

Scanner (AC)

High-quality scans are WAY more useful than the shaky pictures I take with my smartphone's camera! Think about what you are going to be doing with the visual conversation afterwards. If it is going to be shared in a highly visible and significant way—via email to a broader range of team members, or posted online on your website or to wiki—then I recommend scanning at high resolution (300 dpi) whenever possible. This will allow people to zoom in on the image and read the detail, which does not work as well when "Mary Anne with the Shaky Hand" (me!) snaps pics with her phone![5]

Digital Camera (AD)

Photos taken with your smartphone's digital camera are okay for quick "selfie" quality images or conversations. However, these images are often low-resolution and can tend to warp or fisheye. Digital camera photos are great for "working" images or for when you want to pass images along quickly to conversation participants.

A Look at Your Own Tool Kit

You just got a peek inside my professional kit, but you don't need to have everything I do in order to engage in your own visual conversations! Here is a cheat-sheet list for building your own kit, one marker at a time.

Are you ready to try your hand at the big paper, but don't want to spend a lot of money on stuff? Go to your local art or office supply store and pick up the following items:

- **Paper of your choice:** This can be a sketchbook, flip chart, or roll paper—whatever is most appealing for you. (You may find it easier to start on the smaller side and work your way up to larger sizes.)
- **Non-toxic markers:** A water-based marker kit is inexpensive and comes with a variety of colors to play with. Plus, if the ink gets on your hands, it is easier to wash off! (Check to see if their ink bleeds through the paper you chose, though!) You can also use a set of flip chart markers, which are a bit more "fumy" but they should not bleed through your paper.
- **Roll of artist tape:** Use w to secure pieces of paper to the walls or table as needed.

Overthrowing the Ruler

I tend to avoid using rulers in my visual conversations, but you may want to have one on-hand for drawing straight lines and other edges. I leave it out of my kit, along with other formal shape-making gear such as protractors and compasses, because great conversations are very free flowing and I want to echo this flow in the drawing. When I start to create lines with a ruler, I have to go get the ruler, align it, eyeball it, draw the line, put the ruler away, and so on. This process tends to take people out of the flow of the conversation, so I avoid it!

Draw Forth Tip: Match the precision of drawing to the precision of the conversation process. Conversations are informal exchanges of information, and your drawings can help remind people of this. It can also take the pressure off their feeling like they need to get precise on the tiny details before it is time to do so!

There is no hard and fast rule as to what you should place in your visual conversationalist toolkit, only that you get the tools you want to play with. The more appealing they are to you, the more likely you will want to break them out and actually use them! Once you have a basic kit, you can add in additional components to make the kit uniquely yours.

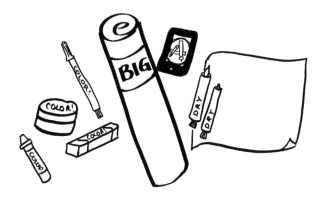

- If you love color, consider getting a set of pastels, crayons, or other markers in a variety of widths and hues.
- If you work with larger teams, consider getting yourself a big roll of paper to play with! (There is nothing like a visual conversation written large across an entire wall. So powerful!)
- If you are more of a digital person, explore different drawing apps like Paper, Brushes, or Sketchbook Pro.
- If you have whiteboards in your office or have more of a whiteboard culture at work, get your own set of dry erase markers in a variety of sizes and some portable cling-on whiteboard sheets. I love putting these sheets on the table for visual conversations: they save paper and they are reusable!

ACTIVITY: YOUR Visual Conversationalist Kit

Now that you have an idea of the different tools and resources out there, let's draw up a list of items you want try for yourself. Use the space below to draw a picture of you with your own awesome visual conversationalist toolkit!

Whether you are a fan of paper, love the whiteboard, or can't keep off the digital stuff, the only way to ultimately find out which tools are the best fit for your particular style and needs is to try a variety of them out and see which ones work best for you! And whatever works best for you is Good Enough!

Internal Tools: What You Bring to the Conversation

In addition to external tools, internal tools are what you bring to the table that you can leverage in yourself, as well as others. Your internal tools include things that allow you to receive and communicate the information you work with. For example, you will need your eyes, ears and mind's eye to visualize what is being talked about. You will also need a way to actually draw things and some "hand-eye coordination" to pull it off. The good news is, you already possess these internal tools and in many cases already have them working for you!

Your Brain is Your Best Tool

← My Brain (Not anatomically correct..)

The visual language you are about to learn is going to be both new and, at the same time, intrinsically familiar to you. Yes, it is true: you already know more of this language than you may realize. In fact, your brain draws upon it all the time!

Before we begin to build our visual language with the basics, let's briefly explore the basics of the brain. Did you know your brain is highly geared for processing visuals?

- 75 percent of your sensory brains are dedicated to visual processes, and
- Over 2/3 of your brain as a whole is used for visual processes.[6]

This knowledge, coupled with the very human desire for story and metaphor, highlights the fact that our brains are complex processing machines. So, as it turns out, your brain works largely on visual inputs and craves to know what happens next so it can make meaning from it.[7]

We may all learn in different ways, but one thing we ALL have in common is that we respond to visuals. It is simply how we are built. Here is the super-cool part: our brains are also wired to mirror what we see other people do!

Caring for your Internal Tools

Remember, you already know what it feels like to be in a great conversation. Simply bring that experience into your visual conversations to make it something special!

When engaging in a visual conversation, make sure that ALL your tools are ready and well cared for. This includes YOU!

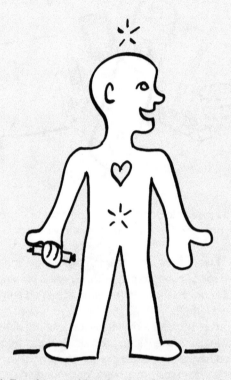

Mind's Eye: Open, unbiased and ready to imagine how ideas can be visually represented
Head: Clear and present
Ears: Open and ready to hear
Eyes: Well-rested and focused
Mouth: Opened thoughtfully
Neck and Jaw: Relaxed
Shoulders: Pulled back and relaxed
Arms: Open and warmed up
Heart: Ready to be of service to the group
Hands: Stretched and warmed up, ready to move, armed with a marker and passing markers to others
Belly: Fed but not over-fed
Gut: Trusted
Body: Loose, limber, alert, fueled and well rested
Butt: In gear!
Knees: Bent, not locked
Feet: Grounded

Monkey See, Monkey "Do"

Think back to when you were five years old. I'd bet dollars to donuts that you drew pictures of some sort or another. These drawing experiences are stored as memories in your limbic brain and neocortex working together.

Thanks to these memories—and a unique type of neuron in our brains—when we watch someone draw images in front of us, our brain thinks it is drawing these images as well. This neurological phenomenon helps us feel a greater sense of ownership of the idea being drawn because our brain thinks we co-created the drawing, even if we never actually contributed a single line.

Here is how it works:

Our brains have something called mirror neurons. These neurons fire when we watch someone engage in an activity we can relate to, both physically and emotionally.[8] This is because we have a memory of doing the activity ourselves somewhere in our brains. For example, when we eat a hamburger our brains light up with a certain activity pattern that says, "eating a hamburger."

When we watch someone else eat a hamburger, our own brains light up with this same "eating a hamburger" activity pattern. Our brain uses its mirror synapses to connect with past experience and responds as if we were eating the hamburger ourselves!

Consider these mirror neurons in the context of visual conversations or visual communication. Do you have physical and emotional experiences putting together super-slick presentation slide decks or computer-generated infographics? If you have never actually assembled a super-slick slide deck or a groovy computer graphic, then you don't have this prior experience to draw upon. This is why when we see these slick presentations and images, they may look cool, but they leave us feeling distant and fairly flat. It is not "our" image; it is someone else's.

Now consider someone drawing out these ideas in front of you, creating simple images—stick figures and the like—to capture the essence of the conversation. Suddenly your brain says, "Hey, I have drawn stick figures before! Sure, it was when I was five years old...but still!" Suddenly, your mirror neurons kick in and it is as if YOU are drawing out these ideas, even though you are really just watching them being drawn. Suddenly, you are co-creating the drawing—all thanks to the mirror neurons in your brain.

As long as you have a frame of reference for engaging in an activity (like drawing stick figures when we were kids), and you see someone else engage in this activity (like drawing ideas during conversations), your brain acts as if you were doing the activity yourself!

This is great news! Your brain is naturally wired to tap into visual language: **all it needs to do is tap back into these memories of when you were five, drawing pictures of your ideas**. Heck, you are just leveraging your natural talents!

> *"The law of perceptual problem solving...may have evolved to ensure that the search for visual solutions is inherently pleasurable rather than frustrating, so that you don't give up too easily."*
> **V.S. RAMACHANDRAN**

Now Draw Forth!

Although having the right physical tools is important, what is more important is how you choose to show up for a visual conversation. When you show up to a visual conversation healthy, whole, well rested, fueled and focused, you are showing up ready to support the conversation and put your tools to good use!

Draw Forth Tools-of-the-Trade Tips

- Have plenty of markers on the table for folks to join in the visual conversation.
- Consider having toys and other items in the room for your kinesthetic learners, creating a creative environment.
- Use color for structure and keep it simple so you don't distract from the discussion.
- Invite drawing-shy participants to use large sticky notes to capture and share their ideas.
- As you move forward and start drawing, don't worry about detail. People's brains fill in the detail in imperfect drawings, allowing them to be more engaged.
- Not every medium is right for every type of visual conversation. Pick your medium's size and surface based on the needs of the conversation. (Small group, small is okay. Large group? Go large! Distributed group? Go virtual, etc.)
- Keep all of your visual conversationalist tools in tip-top condition: this includes you! Rest, eat, stay hydrated, and move.

- Remember: every brain in the room is automatically on your side during a visual conversation because every brain is wired for visuals!
- It sounds silly, but pay attention to what you eat before starting a visual conversation. The last thing you want is your stomach urgently calling you away right when you are in the thick of things! (Seriously!) Eat foods you know agree with you.
- Keeping your markers organized and easily at hand makes drawing visual conversations a delight. Pick up a caddy to store your favorite markers right where you want them, and bring them along with you to meetings and other opportunities for visual conversations. Just making them visible becomes an invitation to draw out ideas.
- Experiment with basic tools first. Don't spend a ton of money up front. Take yourself on a field trip to your local art supply or craft store and try out the different markers and papers they have available. Buy a basic kit and live with it for a while. As you discover what you want, need, and absolutely love, add to your basics and upgrade to your "pro" tools of choice.
- Make sure your marker caps are firmly on at the end of every visual conversation when you are packing up your gear. Test and refill your markers before every visual conversation. It sucks when you grab your favorite marker, only to discover it dried out because the cap was not quite on.

4

Visual Language 101

Ensuring that your external and internal tools are in good shape is a key component of being able to draw out ideas. However, now you are about to delve into perhaps the most important tool you will leverage during visual conversations—visual language itself.

As you will see, the great news is, you already innately know how to do this! Consider what you have already been doing as you have made your way through this book: you have worked through exercises and activities, jotting down notes. You may have even discussed ideas from this book with others! Being able to do all of this requires you to have a language with which to express your ideas. Which clearly you do!

The visual language you will use in your conversations is comprised of five main components. As it turns out, these five components overlay quite nicely onto the five basic building blocks of the language you use every day:

The Five Building Blocks of Visual Language

1. **Letters = Strokes & Shapes**

2. **Words = Icons**

3. **Sentences & Syntax = Composition**

4. **Accent = Style**

5. **Usage = Visual Conversation**

Let's explore each of these building blocks and how they are used a bit more.

1. Letters = Strokes & Shapes

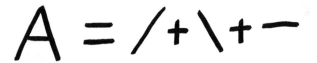

Letters are simply shapes with assigned meanings that a culture agrees upon. For example, we can all agree that an "A" is a vowel with an "a" shape and a certain sound. They are the building blocks of our words. We combine them, along with their corresponding sounds, to make words.

It is the same thing with visual language. Only, instead of letters, we have shapes. The amazing trick is: **If you can draw these, you can draw anything!**

The Roman alphabet has 26 letters:

ABCDEFG
HIJKLMNOP
QRSTUV
WXYZ

In contrast, your visual alphabet only has a handful of lines and shapes: dot, dash, line, curve, spiral, squiggle and angle[1]

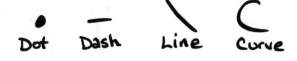

These basics combine to create eight more advanced shapes: triangle, rectangle, square, arrow, star, circle, oval and cloud.

These basic strokes and shapes are the building blocks for everything you draw—from stick figures to the Sistine Chapel! Once you can draw these, you can draw anything.

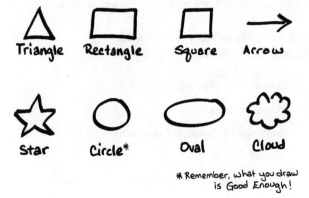

The Sound of Shapes

Did you know that shapes have sounds? Take a look at these two shapes. Which one do you think is named Kiki? Which one do you think is named Bouba?

If you think Kiki is the pointy-figure and Bouba is the blobby-figure, you are not alone. In studies throughout the world, over 98% of people follow this pattern and name the sharp-edged figure Kiki.[2] This is great news because it reinforces the knowledge that people's brains are wired to assess shapes and respond in similar fashions.

Even the way we name things is not completely arbitrary. Rather, something called Synesthesia comes into play. Synesthesia is "the creation of a sense impression relating to one sense of the body by stimulation of another sense or part of the body."[3]

Huh? As it relates to our figures above, it is when we associate similar sounds with similar shapes. "Kiki" sounds "sharp" to our ear, so our minds automatically think, "Oh, the sharp-sounding name must go with the sharp and pointy-looking figure. Since 'Bouba' sounds round and soft, this word must go with the shape that looks round and soft."

So, what does this mean for the lines and shapes you will draw during your visual conversations? The energy and sentiment communicated in a drawing can mirror the energy and sentiment you express in an idea or conversation. More than this, your choice of line and shape will—to a certain degree—communicate additional meaning to your participants because of this synesthesia effect.

You can really grab the room's attention by matching the sense impression of the idea in the room with the strokes and shapes that best embody the "sound" or "feel" of the idea. Why? Because it will communicate the emotions and energy the participant's brain automatically recognizes and registers.

Visual Communication Clues

I've learned a few things from the Godfather of Graphic Facilitation, David Sibbet, over the years. One of them is that the experience of drawing can actually provide participants with clues to the drawing's meaning and information:[4]

POINTS say "Look here, I am different!" They stand out on a white page and draw you eye in.

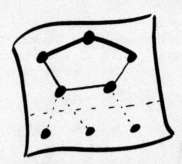

LINES say "connect" or "separate." They are about relationships. Heavy lines feel like stronger relationships, and dotted lines feel like weaker relationships or even separation.

ANGLES say "active change." Angles are lines that actively change direction They are energetic, and angles placed around a point can illustrate an explosion.

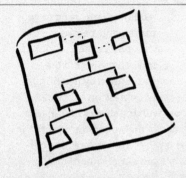

SQUARES and **RECTANGLES** say "formal organization." Solid and sturdy, they are the perfect symbols for buildings and organizational functions.

HOLLOW ARROWS in combinations say "active organization," putting together the meaning of the angle and the square: formal organization undergoing active change.

SPIRALS say "dynamic unity" or "possibility." If you make them more circular, your spirals lean toward unity or even the adjacent possible.[5] If you draw them like tornadoes they suggest more dynamism.

CIRCLES say "unity" pretty much the world over. It feels like you are gathering related things together when you make a circle, just like King Arthur's Round Table.[6]

CLOUDS say "possibility." They contain forming thoughts, bigger picture questions, and other nebulous or emerging content waiting to come into full form.

Practice Time!

In the space below, practice drawing the following strokes:

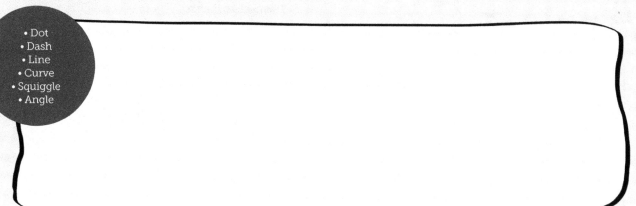

- Dot
- Dash
- Line
- Curve
- Squiggle
- Angle

Now, using the images as a guide, practice drawing the following shapes:

- Triangle
- Rectangle
- Square
- Circle
- Oval
- Star
- Arrow
- Cloud

What other shapes can you think of? Play with drawing different shapes and strokes.

My own shapes and strokes:

Woo! That was hard! (Not really!) See? You were a visual alphabet master and didn't even know it!

Now let's put your visual alphabet to work in the next section.

2. Words = Icons

Apple = 🍎

Just as we combine letters to create words, we combine strokes and shapes to create pictures and visual icons that represent ideas and concepts. People have been doing this for tens of thousands of years. Even our ancestors created cave paintings of important icons in their daily life:

- **Animals**
- **People**
- **Themselves (hands)**

These icons held rich meaning for their creators and for the folks they were created for. Icons can be the same for you as well.

When communicating visually, your icons are your words. You will be communicating with icons to represent the things most important to you. Simply combine basic lines and shapes to create an icon to visually represent a person, place, thing, or concept.

A Basic Visual Vocabulary

When I engage in visual conversations, certain icons tend to keep popping up:

Person

Group of People

Light bulb = idea

Heart = passion

Target = goal

Speech bubbles = literal comments

Arrows = to indicate flow and direction

Computers/Laptops = to frame online services, e-courses, etc.

Faces = to indicate emotion and identity of participants

Radiating lines = to indicate energy of a thing or person

Stars and spirals = to indicate creative processes

Stars = to indicate a "thing" without defining it

Boxes = to frame sections of information

Calendars = to denote important dates and flows

Papers = to indicate printed deliverables

Sunrise = vision, desired future state

Landscape = environment or process over time

Spirals = emerging

Globe = International, holistic

What icons do you think would pop up in your own iconography or visual vocabulary? Let's find out!

Practice Time!

Combine strokes and shapes from the last section to create the following icons:

Person
- Stick figure
- Star person
- Rectangle person
- Squiggle person

Building
- House
- Office
- Neighborhood
- Downtown

Landscape
- Path up the mountain
- Land and shore
- City and country buildings
  (offices, homes, farms)

Conversation markers
- Speech bubble
- Thought bubble
- Idea light bulb

Connectors and Emphasizers
- Arrow
- Flag
- Bullets

 Draw Forth Tip: If you are not sure how to draw a particular icon, check out the Good Enough drawing tutorials at my website: jeannelking.com/goodenough!

From Concrete to Abstract: going deeper with your visual vocabulary

Some icons are easier to draw than others. When we are drawing things that are real and tangible to us, we tend to have an easier job whipping these up:

When we start drawing more abstract things, such as representation of feelings or ideas, it can become a bit more challenging. After all, I have seen a cup of coffee LOTS of times, but what about more complex nouns or concepts? How would you draw "innovation?" Or a "paradox?" This becomes a bit harder because: (1) we don't have something we are literally representing; and (2) as a result, the idea can take many different forms for many people.

Paradox   Pair of Docs

So what do you do when you are in the middle of a visual conversation, you have to represent a more abstract concept, and you have NO idea how to draw it? Here are two approaches you can take:

1. If it is a new word for you and you have no idea how to draw it, you can **ask the person** who said it how it might look to them and how we might represent it in this conversation. This is a great way to engage folks, plus they get to contribute to your emerging visual vocabulary, which is awesome!

2. If it is a new word for you, you have no idea how to draw it and you can't (or don't want to) disrupt the conversation to ask how it could be visually represented, then **don't worry about it!** Words are visual representations, too! Simply write out the word itself in

letters (or even its abbreviation) and keep on going. It is more important to capture the core content and context than it is to miss part of the conversation while trying to figure out which visual word to use to represent it.

I often hear, "But Jeannel, I don't know how to draw everything that comes up in a conversation. Sometimes I don't know what to do because I don't want to use words."

> **Draw Forth Tip:** Words are images, too! Your choice of font can enhance the mood of the conversation. Think of Kiki and Bouba when choosing a font to write in: try using a spiky or sharp font for edgy ideas, and a round or flowing font to make ideas inviting and approachable.

I use words all the time in visual conversations! It is more than okay: it is necessary! Your words help to establish and clarify meaning for your group. When you don't know how to visually represent a thing, focus on capturing the gist of it instead. Write it down. You can always go back to it and play with visualizing it later in the conversation. DON'T stop the conversation or derail its flow. It is more important to capture these ideas before they have flown by!

Another thing you can do with words is make the word more "visual" by infusing the way you write it with meaning! Take the following words:

Stretch   Grow

Stress   Forward

You could simply write them as-is, as I did above. Or you could help the shape of the word better communicate its meaning:

STRETCH   GROW

STRESS   Forward

Now you try it! How could you represent the following words so that their shape helps communicate meaning?

- Drop
- Big
- Tiny

- Expand
- Narrow
- Leverage

Visual Vocabulary On the Fly

Not sure if people recognize what you draw to represent something? Here is a hint: talk through your drawing AS you draw. When you describe what you draw, you are assigning meaning and context to it that others can remember and relate to. Here are two simple examples:

1. **We have a problem with a big ol' bunny eating our vegetable garden. Here is the bunny and here is our garden.**

2. **Joey Jo Jo's donkey escaped and is out wandering the desert. Here is the donkey and here is some sagebrush.**

Did you know what I was talking about in both of the above images? Even though the images are exactly the same, you can help clarify and assign meaning to them by bringing your voice into the conversation!

Remember: we co-create and establish meaning when we draw images together. Plus, our mirror neurons kick in as we watch the drawing being created and say, "Yep, this is totally a donkey and we just drew it!"

ACTIVITY: Finding Your Words

Remember our ancestors from the start of this section? They drew (or painted) images that were important to their lives and communicated key moments and priorities.

What are the icons that are most important and useful to you? Start developing your own visual iconography to draw upon by doing the following:

1. Keep a notebook with you throughout your workday.
2. As you write emails, speak with your teammates or attend meetings, pay attention to the words that keep cropping up during these conversations. For example, when I worked in sea turtle conservation, we tended to talk about sea turtles, communities, fishermen, sharks, ecotourism, and monitoring nesting sites, to name a few. Collect words on your own list until you have at least 10.
3. Once you have a page of words commonly used during your conversations, sit down and look at them. Which words are more basic or fundamental to the business you are communicating about? Which words are more advanced or sophisticated? Which words represent things, and which words represent actions? Get a feel for the common themes in your conversations at work.
4. Pick the top five most basic, most-used words on the list.
5. Convert those five words into a set of basic icons that you can draw.
6. Practice drawing them until you can do so without thinking about *how* to draw them.

Practice drawing those five basic visual icons to represent your words, until you get comfortable drawing them at the drop of a hat.

The next time you are in a meeting or conversation and taking notes for yourself, try drawing those words instead of writing out the words in your notes. See where this simple shift in note taking can take you!

Draw Forth Tip: Not sure how to draw your idea for a particular icon? Not coming up with a good icon idea for your word? Try my go-to process for when I am not sure what I want to draw, or when I am not sure how to draw it:

- Go on the Internet
- Google "word" + clipart
- Select the "images" window to only display images as results
- Peruse images until you see one that really resonates with how you would like to communicate your idea.
- Pick it and draw it your way!

3. Sentences & Syntax = Composition

The apple doesn't fall far from the tree. =

Syntax? What's that again? (After all, it may have been a few years since your last English class.)

The dictionary defines syntax as "the arrangement of words and phrases to create well-formed sentences in a language."

The composition of your visual conversation will be the way you arrange and order your drawings as you create them. These compositions act as your sentences and syntax.

For this section, let's turn to my friend Dan Roam.[7] He has laid out a terrific way to think about how you can arrange your drawings to create well-formed visual sentences. And if a system ain't broke, don't fix it! (Thanks, Dan!)

Dan taught me that, just as there are six different types of information people communicate, there are six different ways to visualize this information:

Dan's Grammar Graph[8]

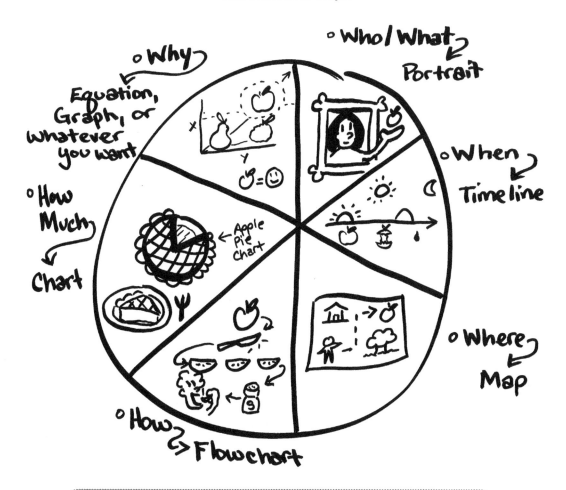

> "Any problem can be made clearer with a picture, and any picture can be created using the same set of tools and rules."
> **DAN ROAM**

Who/What = Portraits

Portraits represent a person or thing. You can think of these as the nouns of our visual language. Names can be general or specific. You can refer to your customer (noun) or your customer, Joe Smith. Either way, a portrait can be drawn to represent him. In the first case, you could draw a generic person to represent your customer. In the second case, you could draw something unique to Joe. Everyone who draws me draws me with curly hair. They don't always even include the glasses! As far as a unique identifier goes, the one with the curly (and red, if it is in color) hair in the drawing is Jeannel.

When to Use: Hear a name, draw a portrait.

When = Timeline

Timelines represent a sequence of events, or the progression of time for a set of data. Instead of representing a person or thing, you would represent the sequence. This sequence could take the form of a story, such as a company's history, or it could take the form of a list of necessary actions, such as the steps you would need to take at specific times to successfully launch your new book. In my case, after I hit a major milestone for a project, like finish a round of edits on my book, I need to get a massage within 24 hours of this accomplishment. (It is just how I write.)

When to Use: Hear a story, draw a timeline.

Where = Map

Maps represent the location and/or relationship of a person, place or thing relative to other people, places, or things. Because we are drawing a map, there is an implied spatial relationship as well: one thing is relative to the next thing. It could be a map illustrating where one might find the salt in your kitchen, it could be the location of the town you grew up in, or it could be your relationship to Alexander the Great within your family tree. It is also helpful to draw a map when you need to group different types of people, places, or things in relation to each other.

When to Use: Hear a list, draw a map.

How = Flowchart

Flowcharts represent the progression of steps or phases in a process without worrying so much about the timing of the execution of these steps. A timeline, for example, indicates that within 24 hours of completing a round of book edits, I need to get a massage. A flowchart, on the other hand, would not be concerned about the timing of the sequence of events, as much as it would focus on the events themselves. In the book-writing example from above, I would simply represent (a) finish round of edits, (b) get massage, (c) start next round of edits.

When to Use: Hear a sequence, draw a flowchart.

How Much = Chart

Charts (or graphs) represent the amount of data relative to other data. Conversations about quantities are prime opportunities to rely on charts to represent the information discussed. As I write my book, I may wonder how many massages I got during the writing process. Or, I may wonder how much more productive I became when I received regular massages.

When to Use: Hear a number, draw a chart.

Why = Equation, Chart, or Whatever Makes the Most Sense to You!

These represent the reasoning and relationships behind process or data results with lots of moving parts or details. These usually come into play when the subject being discussed becomes much more complex. There are multiple factors at play, exerting different effects and influences on a complex situation. (And since this is a more complex piece of our grammar graph, it gets a more complex answer.)

For example, why are sales going up? What are we doing right? It could be any number of things: our social media efforts, our crack sales team, environmental factors, and so on. To represent the increase in sales without representing the diverse factors at play in this situation would paint an incomplete picture.

You can represent the different factors within an equation (e.g. as social media exposure increases, market interest increases, which means that hours per sales call decrease, which means that more sales calls are made within a given period of time, with a higher conversion rate. Or something like this.) You could also represent this with something called a multivariable plot, which is a graph with three or more types of information represented.

Perhaps I want to explain why regular massages are a part of my book-writing process. Part of it is because of the stress reduction, part of it is because of the reward factor for achieving goals and milestones, part of it is because I am actually permanently disabled in my dominant arm and massage helps to keep it working well, and part of it is that I am more productive when I'm a happy camper. For all these variables in the mix, I could create some sort of equation or multivariable plot, like so:

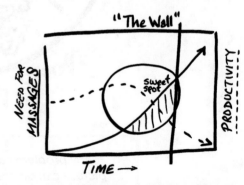

Or I could simply explain why with a series of portraits explaining my "because:"

Sometimes the "why" is pretty straightforward and formulaic. Other times, it's not. Because of this, "why" can be a combination of all of the above options to create a visual explanation for a complex thing.

When to Use: Hear a "why," draw whatever makes the most sense to you!

4. Accent = Style

I am a native Californian, born and bred. When I graduated from high school I went to Marine Corps boot camp in Parris Island, South Carolina. I still remember meeting my fellow recruits on the first day at base. After speaking with me for a moment, they always said, "you're from California, aren't you?" And I would respond, "Oh my Gawd! Like, how did you know?" In my mind I (of course!) sounded "normal," and everyone else around me spoke in these amazing Southern accents.

Everyone has some level of accent. Yours might be a delightful twang or turn of a phrase that is uniquely you. Whatever it is, it is your own speaking style and it is wonderful. It is part of what makes you, who YOU are. It also grows and evolves over time. While I take pride in my California heritage and accent, every now and again you will hear a twinge of a Southern accent in my speech. (Thank you Paris Island!)

Just as you have your own speaking accent, you also have your own drawing accent and style. These styles are what make your work YOURS.

Everyone draws in their own style. However, just about everyone I know also tries to emulate someone else's style to some small degree, or thinks someone else's style is better than theirs . . . again, to some small degree.

For example, I love my loose and joyful cartoony style of drawing. It is how I drew in junior high school, and I have gotten really good at drawing quickly in this style. However, I also LOVE the drawing styles of Mark Monlux and Lloyd Dangle: both professional cartoonists and illustrators. There are times where I can pick up on their styles, or "accents" while drawing, and I see common elements: we all use strong black lines and tend to come from an ink-and-color aesthetic. (They also create comics and I love comics!) Their work is wonderful; I could look at it all day long. (And I have, although I have not exactly told them this. Except I guess I just did. I love you guys!)

However. While I adore their drawing styles, I would never try to turn my drawing style into theirs. Why? Because their styles are just that: THEIR styles! We already have a Mark and a Lloyd in the world. The world does not need me to pretend to have someone else's accent; the world needs me to show up using my own visual voice! Why? Because—truth be told—my visual voice is pretty awesome. Nobody else has it and nobody else ever will.

The same thing is true for you. Your style, your unique way of drawing out ideas and expressing visual metaphors, is unique to YOU. Don't wipe it out for a bland, generic, TV news anchor-like non-accent. And *please* don't train it out of you to look like some other person's—or company's—style.

Don't lose your accent. It is what makes you YOU!

> *"Create your own visual style...*
> *let it be unique for yourself and yet identifiable for others."*
> ORSON WELLES

ACTIVITY: Discover Your Accent

People often describe my visual "accent" or style as whimsical, colorful, joyful, playful, delightful and energetic. It's what they like about it!

At the same time, other folks may find my style to be too childlike or colorful for them. This is cool with me, because I am a gal who owns her visual accent with pride!

What type of person are you? What does your visual accent look like?

- Colorful and dynamic?
- Charming and simple?
- Technical and precise?
- Clean and monochromatic?
- Vivid and fun?
- Messy but effective?

Complete the graph based on the amount each style characteristic resonates with you. And yes, contradictions are just fine! (You can see my own style graph at jeannelking.com/drawforth/resources to see what I mean.)

There is no one "right" style: only your style! Your personality comes through on the page just as it does when you speak. The more familiar you become with your own unique style or "accent," the more comfortable you will become with it, the more you will love and appreciate it, the more you will bring it to the table when you draw...and the more others will love it too!

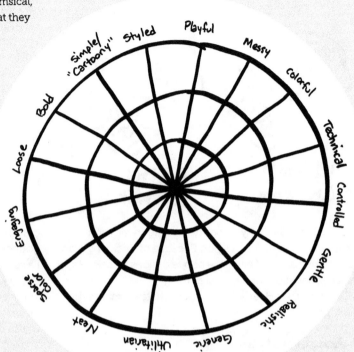

> "Be yourself. Everyone else is taken."
> **OSCAR WILDE**

---

5. Usage = Visual Conversation

At this point, you have the basics of visual language at your fingertips. You can draw strokes and shapes and combine these into icons to represent your ideas. You can also combine icons in various patterns to represent more complex information: who, what, when, where, how, how much, and why. You also have recognition of (and I hope a growing appreciation for) your unique accent or visual style. This is all well and good, but to paraphrase a SoulCollage® friend of mine, to learn this visual language and not use it is a bit like preparing a wonderful meal and not eating it![9]

Your real-time co-creation of drawings becomes visual conversation between you and your participants. This is where people truly start to feel seen and heard, where the conversation comes alive and where people get to fully engage and own what is created. In short, this is where the magic happens. This practice is so important; we are going to spend the entire next chapter exploring it in depth!

Now Draw Forth!

One of the most valuable benefits of visual language is that it helps you effectively communicate ideas in a less intimidating way. Logic, structure, and simple strokes help shape your drawings. Just like you build words out of letters, you can build icons from simple, standard shapes. Just as you would string words together out of letters, you can now string your images in any desired order to communicate different types of meaning.

After all, effective communication is why we learn any language. It is one thing to know what the word is for "bathroom" in a foreign language. It is another thing to know how and when to use this word appropriately, or to understand what someone says in response to your question about where the bathroom is! In the visual language world, usage can become conversational.

Draw Forth Tips to Bolster Your Visual Language Skills

- Just a simple representation is all it takes to get a point across. KISS: Keep It Simple Stick-Figure-Master!
- Talk while you draw to expose your thinking.
- Content is KING. When all else fails, capture the content and embellish later.
- If you don't know how to draw something, look at the shapes involved in it, and draw these. A primitive house is a square(ish) with a triangle on top for the roof. A car can be two circles for wheels and a rectangle or half-circle on top for the car body.
- Think about the order of building an image. Which shape starts the image? Which shape finishes it? Which lines will be in the way of another if you draw them too early?
- Don't know how to draw something that comes up? Get help! Look it up on your smartphone, or ask the person speaking to say more about how they see their idea.
- Challenge yourself to draw more than portraits and pie charts. Practice describing an idea or concept through all six lenses of Dan's grammar graph!
- Keep a notebook and expand your visual vocabulary (or iconography). Add a new "word" to it every day! (Okay, or every few days!)

PART 3:
Engaging in Visual Conversation

5
Using Visual Language With Others

Visual conversation is the interplay between how your participants show up, how you show up and everything in between. At this point you have the basics of your toolkit (both external and internal) and the essential elements of visual language at your fingertips.

So now what? How will you use your newly developed language skills to engage in conversations with others? And how do you do this without freaking them (or yourself!) out? This is where conversation shapers come in.

Conversation Shapers

Have you ever found yourself in a conversation where you did not know what to say or how to approach the situation? As a new visual conversationalist, you may be in the room facing a blank sheet of paper, thinking, "what the heck did I just get myself into?" (I know I asked myself this during my early days of drawing conversations. Few things were more intimidating to me than facing the blank sheet of paper before a conversation began!)[1] If you think this will be the case for you, then meet your new best friends: conversation shapers!

Conversation shapers are the basic visual templates and spatial strategies you can bring to the table to help you shape your drawing of the conversation as it occurs. It gives you a framework and filter through which to listen and reflect the conversation.

After a while, you will become so familiar with these templates and strategies that you will be able to mix-and-match them according to what you are hearing in the conversation. This blank page that was once so intimidating will become a liberating playground and your new best friend!

As you begin to draw out ideas with others, some participants may feel a bit nervous about joining you in a visual conversation. After all, they may not think they can draw, and the thought of drawing with you may push them beyond their comfort zone. However, you and I know that the results are so powerful and the benefits are so good, it is well worth inviting these folks into the visual conversation. So, how can you do this in a non-threatening way that eases them into the visual conversation? Conversation shapers can help! They introduce an interactive, visual aspect to the meeting or conversation without requiring folks to actually draw things themselves (unless, of course, they really want to)!

Basic Spatial Strategies for Shaping Conversations

Remember David Sibbet from chapter 4? He also showed me that there is a logical progression of how we tend to draw forth insights from visual conversations.[2] They include the following seven formats:

1. POSTER = "Focus on THIS!"

I was a child of the '80s and I had a poster in my bedroom of Billy Idol that I ADORED. (Specifically, it was the Rolling Stone cover of Billy Idol wearing chaps. Oh my!) One of my guy friends had a poster in his garage of Heather Locklear—you know, THAT poster with Heather in the hot pink bikini. Another friend of mine loved cars and had a poster of a Porsche 911 in his room. Another friend had the quintessential kitten-hanging-from-a-branch "Hang In There!" poster up on her bedroom door.

Regardless of which poster you might have had in your room, they all served the same purpose: to get you to focus on one thing. This remains true today. The primary purpose of a poster is to place focus on a key point. This can range from one point, which is typical, to a few points at most.

In your work as visual conversationalist, you can use the power of the poster to train attention onto a single point or idea by drawing a single, punchy image. This makes the image stand out from everything else, calling for attention.

The poster corresponds to your dot or point—it says, "Look here!"

2. LIST = "Order Prevails"

The primary purpose of a list is to bring order to multiple pieces of data or information. I'd bet dollars to donuts that you have created a list at least once in your life.

   Whether it is a to-do list, a list of resolutions, a shopping list, or even a list of possible baby names, the creation process is essentially the same: you think of the information and line it up on the page, top-down. The items might be in random order, order of importance, alphabetical order, or something else. But simply from being in a list, order is brought to the information. This is also one of the easiest formats to use when drawing conversations, because our spoken speech is typically linear.[3]

> **The list corresponds to your lines—it says, "These things are connected!"**

3. CLUSTERS = "Compare and Contrast"

The primary purpose of a cluster is to initially sort and organize different information. When I use sticky notes, I cluster A LOT. After brainstorming ideas by writing one idea per sticky note, I put them all on the wall. Then I take a look at the ideas and start to cluster them into like groups to start making meaning and identify patterns in the ideas. Which ideas are similar to others? This is how you leverage clusters for visual conversations as well.

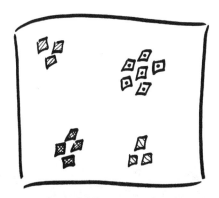

> **Clusters correspond to our angles—they say, "These things are actively changing and organizing!"**

4. GRIDS = "Formalize and Compare"

The primary purpose of a grid is to contain and constrain ideas within a number of categories. Any time you are on the Internet comparing software subscriptions or membership levels, you are likely looking at the information through a grid. For example, software options may be listed out with their features and benefits listed in categories below each option. This grid format allows you to focus on the key features or ideas you value over others.

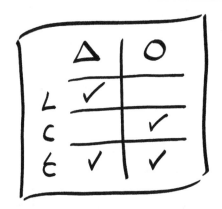

> **Grids correspond to your squares—they say, "These are formally organized now!"**

5. DIAGRAMS = "Parts are Related/Linked to a Whole"

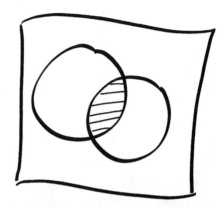

The primary purpose of a diagram is to show how things come together or parse apart. If you think about it, you have been working with diagrams for most of your schooled life.

When I was in high school, my science teacher had us diagram the anatomy of a dissected frog. (Ugh!) In English, we had to diagram sentences to understand how they were constructed. (Double ugh!) When we draw a diagram, we are illustrating a whole by its parts, typically illustrating its appearance, structure or workings. Nowadays, I diagram business models and projects, which I find WAY more interesting and fun![4]

> *Diagrams correspond to your Combos—they say,*
> *"These parts combine to make a whole and this whole deconstructs into parts."*

6. FREE DRAWINGS = "Unique and Dynamic, Expressive"

The primary purpose of an unstructured/free drawing is to express the feelings and dynamics of an idea. Drawings bring ideas to life, whether by representing an idea as a metaphor or translating the energy of an idea into an engaging visual. They translate what the person knows into a visual metaphor they can connect with, relate to, and share with others to pass along the excitement or other emotions.[5] Interestingly, your drawings can also provide the visual environment for other formats (such as lists, clusters and grids) to be used.

> *Free Drawings correspond to spirals—they say, "This is coming together in a dynamic union!"*

7. MANDALAS = "United"

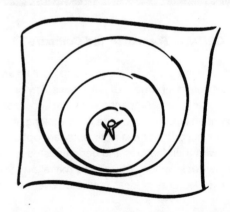

The primary purpose of a mandala is to organize content around a center point to demonstrate unity of information. Mandalas bring everything together into a whole and often circular image. Every aspect of the information is understood as a thing's relationship to the parts AND the whole is drawn forth in your image. A mandala's visual power is in synthesizing complexity into a simple whole.

Have you ever gazed into a mandala? For many, simply looking at the circular arrangement of shapes and patterns brings about a feeling of calm and contentment. In fact, noted psychiatrist Carl G. Jung would ask his patients to draw mandalas as a form of therapy.[6] He reportedly noticed his patients became more focused and relaxed after drawing mandalas. I cannot say I would argue with a side benefit like this when engaging a group of folks in visual conversation!

> *Mandalas correspond to circles—they say, "This is united, this is complete."*

Practice Time!

In the space below, try your hand at applying some of our basic spatial strategies to common conversations you have over the course of the day.

When would it make the most sense to apply these different strategies during your visual conversations?

Note which ones come easiest to you to use, and which ones may want more practice time.

Be sure to give these spatial strategies the time and practice they deserve for you to feel comfortable drawing them up during a conversation, by the way! With experience, you will discover your own favorite go-to conversation shapers. In the meantime, check out the next few pages for some of my favorites.

Jeannel's Top 12 Go-To Conversation Shapers

My preferred style of drawing conversations is free drawing on the blank page, so I can mix and match my favorite conversation shapers based upon the situation at hand. That said, here are the go-to conversation shapers I draw upon the most (in alphabetical order):

1   *Back to the Future, by Jeannel King*

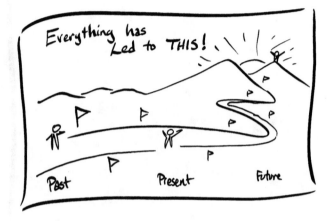

What it does: Reveals the path to our future success, while demonstrating that we have been on this success path all along.

   How to use it: Start with clarifying their vision of future success. Once you have it, "stand" in this future place and look back at how everything they have ever done has led to this future success. Create the timeline of the past into the present day and then continue projecting this timeline into the future until you reach the future vision state. The future timeline outlines the most important milestones to achieve this future state. Seriously powerful stuff!

2   *Business Model Canvas, by Alex Osterwalder et al.[7]*

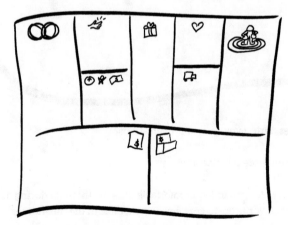

What it does: Shows visually how pieces of a business fit together, how a business makes money, and identifies gaps and deficits in the business model.

   How to use it: Describe the business model through the lens of this canvas, identifying the venture's business proposition, ideal customers, key resources, and other aspects. Once the different components of the business model are fleshed out, you can better understand what it is they are building and how it works.

3   *Ecosystem and influencers, by Jeannel King*

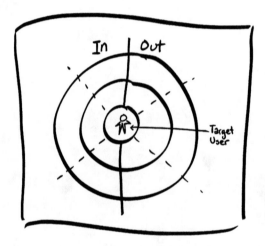

What it does: Identifies interactions and key players in the situation (think "Six Degrees of Kevin Bacon").

   How to use it: The person in the center is your Kevin Bacon—the one you are serving (or wish you were serving). Then add yourself and other key stakeholders to the map, positioning them by degrees of separation from the person in the center. It shows you who else affects and influences the person in the center. It also shows how interactions change when someone else is placed in the center.

4 *Empathy Map, by Scott Matthews*[8]

What it does: Understands others' experiences, getting inside someone else's head and perspective.

How to use it: As a conversation shaper to capture your notes when speaking with someone about their target user or when creating a richer portrait of a marketing persona. Pick a specific person, then document what they think, feel, say, hear, see, and do over the course of their day.

5 *Mind-Map, by Tony Buzan*[9]

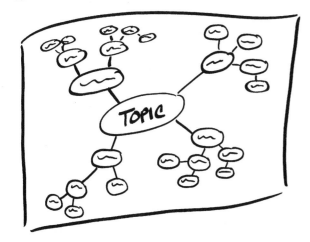

What it does: Brainstorms ideas on a topic, harvests and organizes ideas around a common theme.

How to use it: Place your main topic in the center, and branch off the center in increasing levels of detail for various facets of the topic.

6 *Sticky Notes on the Wall Matrix, based on exercises in Rapid Problem-Solving with Post-It Notes, by David Straker*[10]

What it does: Orders information and weighs choices.

How to use it: First, generate ideas (one per sticky note) and stick them on the wall. Next, move them about, ordering information and weighing choices. Lastly, turn them into a matrix-timeline-flowchart hybrid by moving the sticky notes into a Gantt chart format.[11]

7 *Problem Pizza, by Dan Roam*[12]

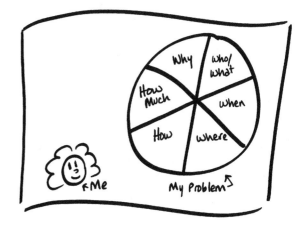

What it does: Understanding and defining a topic from a variety of angles.

How to use it: Start by identifying the problem, challenge, or even opportunity you currently face. Next, draw your understanding of the problem (or opportunity) through these six different lenses to gain a richer understanding of the subject.

8 *Snapshot of the Big Picture, by Patti Dobrowolski*[13]

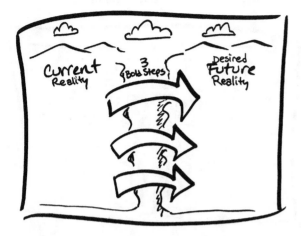

What it does: Shows you your current state, your desired future state and the three bold steps required to move you from your current state into this desired future state.

How to use it: Start by drawing your current state. Be sure to use images and color, and no words. Take a short break, and then draw your desired future state. Lastly, consider the biggest, boldest steps you can take to bridge the gap from where you are to what you want. Write down the three biggest steps in the center.

9 *Storyboard, by Walt Disney*[14]

What it does: Provides a structure for sequential visual storytelling and development. With up to 12 panels to a page, storyboards are great for visualizing stories, sequences and timelines.

How to use it: Storyboards are useful to sequentially order and process content. Draw each stage or sequence of a story one frame at a time. You can also create a new VISUAL story for how a person's response to a situation can change to better match a desired outcome or future state.

10 *Timeline, by Anonymous*

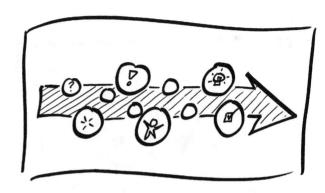

What it does: Order and evolution of a thing, also predicting the future based on the past. Draws forth the story of conversation.

How to use it: Timelines can be used to reverse-engineer a conversation. First, identify the desired outcome and deliverable date, then reverse-engineer the steps to making this deliverable occur in the time you have. You can also use a timeline to define and shape the story of a group's shared history, or to predict the future— both are pretty powerful experiences!

11 *Venn Diagram, by John Venn*[15]

What it does: Similarities, differences and possible effects of interactions between disparate-yet-connected things.

How to use it: Use it to show how different values, ideas or even groups combine. You can see what is lost (or gained) when two groups combine without a third, and you can see what is gained (or lost) when all three groups combine together. Surprisingly insightful stuff!

12 *Concentric Circles Prioritization, by Jeannel King*

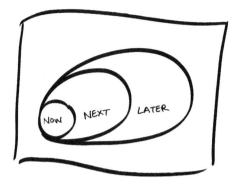

What it does: Provides a framework for prioritizing tasks over an undefined period of time. Separates priorities into stages (immediate, short term, long term).

How to use it: Create three concentric circles. "Now" is the innermost circle. These are the things you need to focus on in the immediate term. Once these are nailed, you can look to the next concentric circle to see what the next stage or phase of a project's needs are. The third and largest circle contains the stage-three items. I like to list items on sticky notes and place the notes in the circles so they can migrate towards the innermost circle and then move out when they are complete.

This is of course by no means a complete list. One of the great things about being a visual conversationalist is that there are many effective visual templates and "conversation shapers" already out there, so you don't have to feel pressured to reinvent the wheel. Learn and master these basics and then give yourself permission to use them in new ways. You may even evolve them to a whole new level!

Giving credit where credit is due

Be mindful when using visual templates. Some templates, such as the Snapshot of the Big Picture or the Business Model Canvas, are freely shared by their creators for you to use. Others, such as visual templates available from the Grove Consultants International, are proprietary approaches and should be attributed as such. If you are unsure whether or not to attribute the source of your visual template, ask the template's creator. Whenever possible, it is always good form to credit the creator of any conversation shaper you use.

Now Draw Forth!

You are now equipped not just with the basics of a visual language, but also with some essential conversation shapers for actually drawing out conversations with others! You are ready to start drawing forth the best in conversations. Congratulations!

Wait, what's that? Still not ready to step up to a blank piece of paper and start drawing with family, friends, colleagues, or even (gasp!) your boss? Never fear, this is what the next section is all about.

But first, here are five tips to help you build your skill and technique, so you feel more confident to draw forth!

Stick Figure Strategist Tips to Bolster Your Technique

- Break out the sketchpad while watching television or listening to the radio. As you listen to the show, play with translating the discussion into our different spatial strategies on the fly. The more you practice translating conversations into these forms, the easier it will be to do it live.
- Look for opportunities in your live conversations where different spatial strategies could be applied. Make a note to yourself about how the spatial strategy could work, then practice drawing it as the conversation flows. Draw it first for yourself if you choose, and then draw it with and for the group.
- If you prepare templates in advance for your visual conversation, don't display them until they are needed, as they can become distracting and lead folks away from the current topic of conversation.
- Learn through the observation of others. In my field we have an acronym for this: "CASE"—copy and steal EVERYTHING! Don't literally steal, of course! Rather, create your own CASE file of images that inspire you and you wish to learn from. Use these images to understand different styles and learn other ways of drawing out ideas. Learn from these inspiring images, and grow into your own style and visual "accent."
- Practice, Practice, Practice! Find a practice buddy with whom to keep your visual conversation skills in play, share images, celebrate with, and even commiserate with on occasion.

6

Facing the Blank Page

One of the most common questions I am asked is: How do you know what to do with the paper during a visual conversation? After all, you don't know what is going to happen as the conversation unfolds, so how are you able to make things work out perfectly on the page?[1]

This question always reminds me of a class I was in, where the instructor had us "play conductor" as we listened to a gorgeous and dynamic piece of music. Later, one of the instructors came up to me and said, "I was watching you during the 'play conductor' session: you were so in the flow of the piece, you must have heard that song before!" As it turns out, I had not. I did, however, share with him that I was raised to think like a musician. You see, my dad was a jazz musician who taught me how to see the patterns in music and, because of this, see what was likely to come next.[2]

So the best answer I can give for the question, "How do you know what to do?" is this: ***It is just like Jazz***.

5 Tenets of Jazz

1. **Know the Basics.**

2. **Know the Patterns.**

3. **Know How to Listen to Others & Follow the Melody.**

4. **Improvise!**

5. **Play the Wrong Note Twice.**

Jeannel's Jazzy Strategy for Playing with the Blank Page

Everyone has different approaches for working a blank page during a visual conversation. As we learned in the last chapter, some of these approaches are shaped by a visual template or spatial strategy. For example, if you want to talk about the history of an organization, you can use a timeline template to shape the conversation. However, the real art of visual conversation comes into play when you start with the *blank page*. This is where you get to be a jazz musician. Learning and mastering these five tenets of jazz will help you also master how to approach the blank page.

Tenet 1: Know the Basics

Knowing how to play your instrument allows you to improvise well with others. You don't need to be Miles Davis to be able to jam with others.[3] You do, however, need to know how to play your instrument. In this case, "playing your instrument" means enjoying a fair level of competency in drawing out ideas in real time so you can keep up with the conversation.

One of my favorite memories growing up is of my dad accompanying silent movies on the organ.[4] Interestingly, he was not always familiar with a movie's plot (and this was in the days before one could simply look up information about a film online). Sometimes he only had a general idea, at best. What he DID have, though, was the ability to play the pipe organ and an ever-expanding library of music in his head as a jazz musician. So as each film's story unfolded as it played on the giant silver screen over his head, my dad could adjust his music to fit the mood and message of the movie. Of course, the more he did it, the better he got at it!

It is easier to improvise when you have a certain level of mastery over your skills. On the other hand, it is hard to improvise with others when you don't know the musical rules of the road, so to speak. For example, if people are going to play jazz in the key of B-flat and you don't know what the key of B-flat sounds like, or how to play within this key, it will be difficult for you to play well with others. Mastery kicks in when you don't have to think about how to play in B-flat: you just do it. Likewise, mastery kicks in when you don't have to think about what you draw: you just draw it and trust it is the right thing to do in the moment.

Tenet 2: Know the Patterns

Music follows a certain structure, just as conversations do. Musicians know if a set lasts 90 minutes, they have to figure out how many songs to play during the set and work from there...improvising as needed.

Similarly, the length of a conversation can provide clues to its structure. If you know you are going to be in a conversation for a certain amount of time, or that a section of a conversation is going to last for a certain amount of time, you can plan your blank sheet space accordingly. Would an 8.5 x 11" sheet of paper be enough to draw out an hour-long conversation? What about a 4' x 8' sheet? Just as music has sections, conversations have sections and you can plan your use of blank space to accommodate these section needs.

Sections also have different levels of importance. The trick is knowing which sections are important to remember from the conversation. For example, a conversation may be scheduled to last all morning and the first half hour or so will be focused on introductions. Time-wise, this is over 16% of your meeting (30 minutes from a 3 hour meeting time). Do you allocate 16% of your white space to capturing what is shared during the introductions? It depends. If the purpose is to build trust and connection within your team, then these personal details and personal shares may be extremely valuable to remember. In this case, this section of the meeting has a heavy weight of importance and you would allocate space for it accordingly. Then again, the introductions may simply be a formality for everyone to know who is in the room and what they bring to the table, with the really important stuff coming during the meat of the conversation itself. In this case, the introduction time is of a lower level of importance as compared to the rest of the meeting and you may not need to dedicate much page space to it at all, if any. In jazz, you can take liberties around the melody (or core content), and you can even put your own style on it, riff off into a blazing jazz solo, or even do a round of solos with your band. But the melody – the core content – holds the highest level of importance. Knowing the core content and purpose of the conversation is your guide.

Tenet 3: Know How to (Listen to Others) and Follow the Melody

A jazz version of a song can sound like it has a set melody when you start to listen to it; then, before you know it, it takes on a life of its own. Well, the same thing can be said for conversations. You may think you are going to spend a certain amount of time talking about topic A, but once you dig into the conversation you discover what we REALLY need to discuss is topic B, and this requires a different amount of time – a shorter or longer conversation session. Being able to listen to others and pick up on these changes in conversation as they occur allows you to adjust your plan for working the paper. You may decide to chuck your initial design strategy, morph it into something else, or even get another sheet of paper to work on, all while staying true to the original purpose (or melody) of the conversation.[5]

Tenet 4: Improvise!

You have probably heard the saying, "Practice makes perfect." Well, let's take this saying to a higher level: "Practice makes pleasure." This phrase can just as easily be applied to your conversations as it can be applied to playing jazz.

Let me explain: The more you do something (whether it is playing jazz or drawing out a conversation), the more familiar you become with how it works, and how you work with it. Practicing by yourself and with others allows you to hone your skills and really jam with the group. When you feel more on top of your game, you can relax and be free to enjoy the process more!

Tenet 5: Play the Wrong Note Twice

There is an old adage in the Jazz world: "If you play a note wrong once, it's a mistake. Play the wrong note twice and it's jazz." In other words, own your own unique approach to music and run with it!

Again, this tenet of jazz can also be applied to visual conversation. In conversation it is about owning your abilities and playing your paper. If you make a mistake, keep going and make it work for the conversation. Use it as a moment to clarify what is being discussed and check for understanding. Or catch the mistake, correct it and keep on going with the conversation.

> "Jazz stands for freedom. It's supposed to be the voice of freedom: Get out there and improvise, and take chances, and don't be a perfectionist—leave that to the classical musicians."
> **DAVE BRUBECK**

ACTIVITY: Visual Jazz

The secret to being able to improvise like a jazz musician is to know how to play your instrument. Once you have this foundation set, and you can trust not having to think about "how" to play, these core skills give you the freedom to play any way you want.

Let's add a bit of jazz to your visual conversation:
1. First, think back to the visual language section when you drew yourself. This drawing is your foundation, the "essence" of you.
2. **Now, draw YOU five different ways in the space below. Start to play with what happens when you draw yourself with really big hair, a different style of body, NO body, or how you show up in your natural state.**

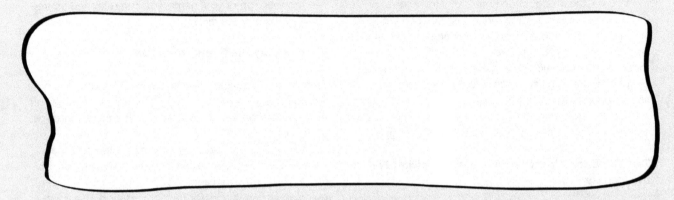

Good job! See how you can take liberties on the shape and yet it is still essentially YOU? Here is what I got when I did this:

As you can see, you don't have to draw something exactly how you think of it or expect it to look, to communicate what it is. Taking liberties drawing shapes gives you the flexibility to imbue images with additional meaning gathered from your conversation, giving your drawings an added level of richness and depth.

Now let's do this with one of these more abstract concepts:
1. Think back to the visual language section, when you drew your home. This drawing is your foundation for what "home" looks like to you.
2. **Now, draw HOME five different ways. Perhaps it is where the heart is, or where you hang your hat. Perhaps it is not a building, but a place or even a planet!**

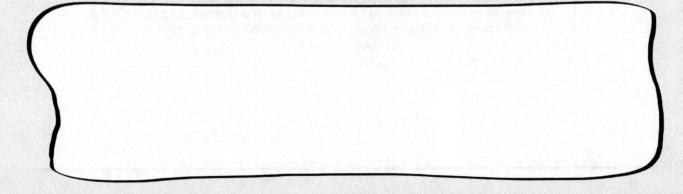

Nice! Here is what I got when I did this:

When you have a basic understanding of what the image looks like to you, and you feel comfortable and strong in your ability to draw this image quickly and easily, then this is the place where experimentation and creativity starts to take root!

One more time, now! Pick your own word, play around with it and draw it five different ways in the space below:

My word: _____

Remember, practice makes pleasure!

The Pattern is Never Perfect

Are you never quite satisfied with your work or efforts, because they don't result in an end product that is absolutely perfect? If so, take a seat on the rug and have a listen.

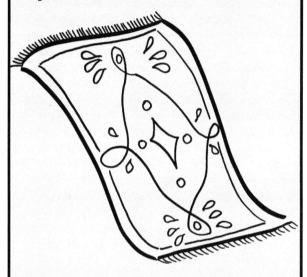

Visual conversations are not just like jazz: they are also a lot like Persian rugs. No two are ever the same and mistakes, both intentional and unintentional, make them more beautiful.

My boyfriend, Jamie, collects magnificent Persian rugs. During one of our first rug-buying outings, we were examining a particularly meticulous and stunning rug when Jamie noticed a few knots out of sync with the rest of the pattern. It seemed odd that everything else about the rug would be so precise and perfect, except for this one small spot.

The shop owner explained to us that in his culture there is a belief that only God makes perfect things, so when rug makers masterfully weave a rug they intentionally include a mistake as acknowledgment to their Creator, who is the only perfect thing.[6] The imperfection was actually a showing of love and respect. When Jamie and I learned this, these mistakes only amplified the beauty—and our appreciation—of the rugs.

So, if you find yourself drawing a mistake in an otherwise-awesome visual conversation, think of it as your own tribute to being human and appreciate the extra beauty the "mistake" can bring to your creation.

To Pre-Draw or Not to Pre-Draw: Strategy & Approach

Pre-drawing is a fairly common practice among visual conversationalists. This is because sketching out a visual template or spatial strategy to work within during a conversation can help you contain, shape and more effectively share thoughts with others. However, they can also commit you to a specific format, leaving you with little wiggle room should the conversation's subject or needs change. Being locked into a visual strategy can make it exceedingly difficult to adjust in mid-conversation.

Do you remember when I said I don't like to be over-prepared? This is true when it comes to pre-drawing conversations as well, and especially after my experience with the Community Education Project I shared with you back in Chapter 2.[7] What this experience, and every one thereafter, taught me is that it is important for me to *pre-plan* my visual conversation strategies, rather than *pre-draw* them. Here is what this looks like for me:

1. First, I find out the agenda and details of the meeting or conversation in advance, including the main logistics and purpose:

Consider the following three criteria when gathering *logistical information*:

- **What is the length of the meeting or conversation?** This will help you to determine how much drawing medium you will need.
- **Where is it going to be held?** This will help you decide which drawing medium to use.
- **Who is going to be there?** This will help you understand the nature of the conversation.

Focus on the following three criteria to get to the heart of the *meeting purpose*:

- **Why are folks coming together and what do they hope to accomplish?** Knowing this will help you get clear on the priorities and outcomes for the conversation...and what to listen for.
- **What is the context and topic of the conversation?** These will help you understand what the conversation is about and why it is important.

- **What is the desired outcome of the conversation?** At the end of the conversation? Beyond the end? This will help you strategize your visual conversation so it may best support your group's work after the conversation ends.

2. Once you have this information, sketch out any ideas you have for visual templates and spatial strategies that could best support the conversation.[8] For example: If this is an initial planning conversation for a team project, they will probably be generating ideas for the next big project. You can support the team's best work by drawing up ways to capture and prioritize the brainstormed ideas. Then you can use a visual template or spatial strategy to structure the team's official decisions and action items moving forward.

3. It is also helpful to spend some time looking online at images related to the topic of conversation and the team's industry.[9] This is a great way to refresh your visual vocabulary and familiarize yourself with specific images or icons you might want to include during the conversation.

4. Once you have this research done, forget it and just show up. Yes, you read this right. Just forget it. And here is why: What people *think* they are going to talk about does not always align with what they will *actually* talk about. So, while it is great to have a strategy in your head you can draw upon, it is best to walk into the actual conversation as a blank slate (and with a blank sheet), so you are ready to hear what is really going on in the actual conversation and reflect it accordingly. This approach will provide you with ideas that can help you shape the structure of the visual conversation as it progresses, yet it will afford you the luxury of disregarding your strategy to adapt to the emerging needs of the conversation.

Like my dad accompanying a silent movie, you will have a general idea of what the conversation's going to be about and a library of resources in your head. This will help you develop an unshakeable confidence in your ability to step up and support any visual conversation as it unfolds.

> *"Jazz is about being in the moment."*
> **HERBIE HANCOCK**

Anatomy of a Simple Strategy for Visual Conversation

- Summarize the main idea or challenge in the headline.
- Create a happy caricature of the person speaking with speech bubbles containing the salient points.
- Highlight small ideas with directional arrows and fun borders or frames.

- Create small images to embody ideas.
- Every opportunity stimulates a new image or graphic.
- Combine the basics—like frames, lines and arrows—with font work.
- Use colors to highlight key elements and make the visual more interesting.

- If you are feeling at all lost, confused, or overwhelmed, simply focus on the melody—the core content—and embellish with visuals later.

Etiquette Guidelines & Tips for Polite (Visual) Conversation

Attribution? Yes or no. Know up front.

In the professional arena, it is sometimes important to attribute specific comments or ideas to specific people. For example, in a board meeting, you would want to state who made a motion and who seconded the motion.

However, in most conversations and group collaborations, non-attribution is not uncommon. What is non-attribution? This is when everyone's ideas are represented without names attached to them, so only ideas are captured on the page. This way, there is no name-weight attached to an idea, so all ideas and contributions are received equally. Even your boss'. (Especially your boss'!)

That said, people have a deep need to know their input has been taken into consideration and incorporated into the bigger picture. As a visual conversationalist, you can help make this happen by putting these five best practices to work:

Five "Drawing Forth the Best" Practices

1. **Use Their Words, Not Yours**
2. **Check for Accuracy**
3. **Listen and Reflect Meaning**
4. **Reflect Back Clearly**
5. **Sign Your Work**

1. Use Their Words, Not Yours

More than practically anything else, people want to be seen and heard. The best way you can show someone that they have been seen and heard is to reflect what he or she said back to him or her. For example, let's say that during a meeting you share information about a flaw in a product's design that could cause problems for production and for client satisfaction. Then let's say you read back the minutes from this meeting and they reflected that you had no faith in the project and thought it was doomed to failure. Would you feel seen and heard at this point? Or would you feel misunderstood? Frustrated? Attacked? Sabotaged, even?

Using people's own words as the verbal content for your visual conversations allows people to literally see they have been accurately heard. If they feel like they have been misunderstood, it is easily caught and corrected in the moment.

2. Check for Accuracy

If you are drawing a visual conversation and someone says something you are not quite clear about, check to make sure you understand things correctly. Your visual conversation can be a great aid for this. By pointing out a specific area you drew – or are about to draw – you can use it as a tool for asking if you have understood the concept correctly. After all, this is going to be the visual artifact participants will refer to for remembering the conversation. It is perfectly appropriate to check for accuracy as you go. Odds are good that, if you did not quite understand something in the conversation, someone else did not get it either and they will appreciate you asking![10]

3. Listen and Reflect Meaning

One of the most effective aspects of visual conversation is its ability to reflect meaning back to the participants. What is meaningful during the conversation? Anything that evokes a response contains meaning that could be worth remembering.

Did someone suggest an idea the team knows is the right course of action, but generates a lot of resistance around the suggestion? This is something meaningful to capture and reflect back to the group! (It can actually help diffuse this resistance and make forward progress easier in the long run—naming an elephant in the room, so to speak.)

Did a shared joke create a stronger sense of bonding or camaraderie in the group? It may be worth capturing a visual reminder as a small image!

The main thing is to capture and reflect the gist of the conversation—what folks will want and need to remember to be able to do their best work moving forward.

4. Reflect Back Clearly

Making certain your visual conversation is clear, focused and simple ensures that no questions will arise when your participants revisit your work later. Remember, you are making visual sense of conversation data and it is important that all participants understand what you are trying to get across. This is a critical factor—and skill—when engaging in visual conversations. (Thank goodness it is also a skill that improves with practice!)

5. Sign Your Work

Finally, always sign your work. I like to sign the bottom right corner of the page with the event's date and my contact information. I do this just in case someone has a question about the conversation and wants something clarified. People involved in the visual conversation usually "get" what has been created, because they were co-creators of its content and were there when it was created. However, it is good business practice to provide participants with a way to follow up with you directly should anything need refreshing or clarification.

For added commitment and to promote ownership of the results of your conversation, consider having all conversation participants sign the drawing of your visual conversation as well. You might be surprised by how powerful an experience this can be for you and participants alike!

What to Do When There is No Meaning

Sometimes, people speak without actually saying much of anything. I call this type of conversation the **Donut**: it may look substantial, but is full of empty calories and is deeply dissatisfying.[11]

A few years ago, I was mentoring two high school students who were about to create a graphic recording for the first time. We were at a school district meeting and the structure was for the district's superintendent to present to the community for a half an hour, followed by a dialogue about proposed initiatives. Before the event started, I reminded my students to listen for and reflect meaning. When the superintendent started his presentation, the students waited, markers at the ready. They waited...and waited. Finally, after about 10 minutes, one of the students turned to me and whispered, "He is not actually SAYING anything, is he?"

"No," I whispered back, "No, he is not." It took the superintendent 25 minutes to finally get to the meat of his point, and I could not have been more proud of these students at the recording wall for recognizing this and waiting it out until the salient point emerged!

Now Draw Forth!

Every time I face the blank page for a visual conversation, I get butterflies in my stomach just like when the curtain is about to go up for a performance. It is scary-exciting (a word I use ALL the time!) and I love it. I love the twinge of fear I feel, because it tells me I am about to do something that pushes me out of my comfort zone and into the unknown.

I don't know what will happen in any particular visual conversation, but once it starts that conversation really does develop a life of its own. Although stepping into this unknown is still a bit scary every time, it is also exciting as all get-out! Like a jazz performance, something wonderful and unique is about to happen. Like a jazz musician, I know how to play my instrument and I know the fundamentals of my "music." I can read my fellow conversationalists and go where the music wants to take us. As you will soon see for yourself, no matter how many conversations you host (even on the exact same topic), just like jazz, they will be different every time.

At this point, I would not be surprised to hear you are probably experiencing some scary-excitement in your belly, too. I hope so! This is a good thing! This energy will help you breathe life and color into your visual conversation "performance." It is energy you can use to draw forth the best in yourself and others while drawing out these ideas in visual conversation. Remember: the way you show up is the way everyone around you gets to show up. But more on this in the next chapter!

Additional Strategies for Approaching the Blank Page

- Be patient and don't panic!
- Remember that points take time to develop and folks may go through a verbal throat clearing.
- Knowing that this happens—and being patient with it—is half the battle!
- Listen for the "wheat" and toss the "chaff."
- If you are not hearing any wheat, and find yourself sitting through a lot of chaff, don't draw anything. Your stillness can be a cue to your conversation participants to check and see if they are still on-track. Invariably someone will say, "Hey, our visual conversationalist here has not drawn anything for a while now. Let's get back on point!"

How to Keep the Visual Conversation Flowing

When conversations shut down, we are no longer able to collaborate, communicate, achieve our outcomes, or take meaningful and directed action towards the results we seek. This is why I no longer "do meetings": oftentimes they provide a space for us to talk "at" each other instead of work "with" each other.[1]

Your work is far too important to be blocked by ineffective communication practices! And while many things can contribute to shutting down conversations, here are five common challenges I routinely see and how you can avoid them:

Five Challenges Around Conversation

1. *Fragmentation of Thought*

There is an old saying: "When all you've got is a hammer, everything becomes a nail."[2] The way we think about our world determines what we see. When we divide our world into separate categories of thought, we fall into thoughts about "us" and "them." As our thoughts fragment, we become the hammer and everything else is the nail—wanting a good pounding. Furthermore, when thinking becomes narrow and limited, "group hypnosis" or "group-think" can kick in, leading to all sorts of assumptions about "problems" and "solutions."[3]

The Fix: Flip your pronouns. When you notice people talking about "us" versus "them", start using "we" for everything to create a more inclusive environment.

Years ago, I was working with a leadership team in a non-profit setting. Well, technically they were a "team." In reality, they viewed themselves as individuals forced to work with people they did not trust and knew were out to sabotage their ability to do good work. It was always, "I needed the information but THEY screwed me over!" So I made one change in how I interacted with them: I spoke only in terms of "we" and "us." It did not matter if we were talking about who let down whom, or who was going to pick up the coffee: I spoke about "us" and "we." The first time I said "we" in a conversation, I remember one of the team members looking at me with a shocked look on her face. You could practically read the thought bubble over her head: "What do you mean 'we' crazy woman?" However, within five minutes, she was saying "we" as well. By the end of the conversation, the entire team was using it. Instead of blaming each other for problems other people had clearly caused, the team was able to see the bigger picture and how they could collectively be successful. A few weeks later, the rest of the organization started commenting how tight-knit this team had become. All because of a simple pronoun change!

2. Taboo Topics

Sometimes our work environment can feel more like a petting zoo with all the elephants, cows, and snakes hanging out there. "Elephants in the Room", "Sacred Cows" and "Snakes in the Grass" mean restrictions are placed on what can be discussed in a conversation. The Elephant is the thing everyone knows but cannot say. The Cow is the thing absolutely off-limits to touch, criticize or change. The Snake is the thing we don't approach because we are afraid we will get bit and die a horrible death. These are cultural animals and those within the culture know to stay away from the Elephants, Cows and Snakes.

When people are unable or afraid to speak openly about something, then critical contributions are lost, information and opportunities are missed and trust erodes. Alternatively, when people are willing to talk about them, these topics often turn out to be critical factors in determining the strategic plan, solving the current problem, creating the team's vision, or developing the team's ability to learn.

The Fix: Point it out. Shine a light on what is not being talked about. Name it. Make it visible. For example, you could say, "I notice we are dancing around this thing. Can we name it?" This does not mean you have to take it on or solve it; simply making it visible allows people to speak to it.

3. Lack of Presence

When we are in a conversation and our attention is divided (i.e. we are checking email under the table or "taking notes" on the computer while hiding behind the screen monitoring sports scores) and we are not truly IN the conversation. We are not even a witness to the conversation. We are present to other things, instead of what is going on in the room.

The Fix: Agree to engage. Establish at the beginning of the conversation how the group is going to stay "together and present" during the conversation. Address the challenge before it has time to show up. This could be accomplished by having all participants place their phones in the center of the table until the conversation has ended or the group is taking an official break. Or, keeping everyone present could be as simple as asking individuals direct, clarifying questions and giving them a few minutes to form group answers.[4] However you decide to best support the group, the key is to keep everyone fully engaged and interacting for the duration of the conversation.

4. Lack of Listening

Keeping people engaged is just a start. Folks also want to be seen and heard when they share their thoughts and feelings with other people or the group. Yet when we are preoccupied with what we are going to say instead of truly keying into what is being said in the moment, we are disengaging from the conversation. Instead of responding to what was actually said, we end up jumping over or (worse!) we dis-acknowledge another's contribution and instead steamroll with our all-important train of thought.

The Fix: Focus on being "together." If you start to catch yourself drifting, shut down technology and train back in on what is being shared.[5] Repeat what others have just said, or do anything that helps you once again become present and attentive to hearing what is being said.[6]

5. Lack of Acknowledgement

Few things shut down contributions in a conversation as effectively as a lack of acknowledgement for people's contributions—or outright theft of these contributions! People care about what they create and generally take pride in being able to contribute. They also want to be seen and heard. Claiming other people's ideas as our own fosters a lack of trust and openness and reluctance to contribute thoughts and ideas to the conversation.

The Fix: Give credit where credit is due. Capture people's ideas up on the board and mirror or connect them back in a timely manner so they feel heard. Depending on the culture of the group (family or business), create an agreement on how you will acknowledge what is being said so everyone feels their contributions are being equally considered. Does it happen perfectly every time? No. Doing our best by taking these steps, though, will allow the group the space they need to address how everyone is to be seen, heard and collectively acknowledged so you can move on with a productive visual conversation.

> *"It was impossible to get a conversation going, everybody was talking too much."*
> YOGI BERRA

Six Conversation Stoppers and How to Handle Them

It is no fun when you are in a great conversation and someone does or says something to shut the whole thing down. This can happen in visual conversations, too!

Etiquette, as we talked about in the last chapter, is important in a visual conversation, not just for the specific things you "do" during conversation, but also for how you "show up." These six visual conversation stopper roles may be easy for anyone in the group to fall into—including you! But how can you recognize when these roles show up? And how can you fix them in the moment?

1. The Interrogator: Interrogators are always looking for ways to fill up a page based on what is on their template, versus what needs to organically emerge from the conversation. They just want to fill up the page and ask questions that barrel along like a Mack truck and fit their template. Their questions are rarely probing, but rather a lot like filling out a form. And boy, are they in a hurry to get this form completed! They are not even listening or talking "with" you: it feels like they are talking "at" you. Such a dissatisfying exchange can leave everyone a bit exhausted!

The Fix: Focus on the "with." Ask open-ended questions and dig deeper based on the responses you receive. Be patient with the process.

2. The Braggart: Braggarts focus on their amazing drawing skills over any content being shared. "See how well I drew this picture of the CEO? Isn't this cool? Don't you love how I drew this idea? Steve Jobs LOVED it when I drew his talk, let me tell you!" (Are your eyes rolling yet?) Instead of the conversation being the focus, the drawing becomes the focus, and it ends up taking everyone off-track.

The Fix: Keep the visual conversation focused on the topics at hand rather than the artistry involved in drawing it out. Have participants draw right along with you. Also, be sure to demonstrate your own Good Enough drawing skills so participants know they don't have to be a "Picasso" or other renowned artist to contribute their best visual thinking.[7] They will share in the belief that what they draw is Good Enough!

3. The Monopolizer: Monopolizers hog the pens or markers, even when others are willing and wanting to add to the visual conversation. They "draw" themselves into the spotlight and won't give it up.

The Fix: Pass the pens and put markers out on the table so participants can easily access them during the conversation. Gather everyone around the paper, along with yourself. Ask others how they visualize the topic or how they would frame it as a metaphor. As people start to share their visuals pass them a marker and invite them to add to the visual conversation. Most importantly, make sure you have created an environment where people feel safe to draw forth their Good Enough ideas!

4. The Interrupter: Interrupters know what you are going to say before you finish saying it and are already drawing your point before you have even made it. They tend to jump ahead in the conversation to the next piece, instead of staying present in the conversation.

The Fix: Put the pen down and listen. If timing is a concern or if the conversation seems to be going off in an unproductive direction, check in with the group and see how everyone would like to proceed.

3. The Know-it-All: Know-it-Alls typically dominate the conversation. They are quick to tell everyone everything they need to know about the topic of conversation. They are rarely interested in other people's opinions: just their own. Know-it-Alls can also push their own agenda while holding the pen, rather than being of service to the group.

The Fix: Ask what other people think, pass the pen to someone else and, most importantly, LISTEN.

> *"You're short on ears and long on mouth"*
> JOHN WAYNE

4. The Intimidator: Intimidators are such great artists they make everyone else feel reluctant to even draw next to them. It may not even be intentional on the Intimidator's part: they simply make others feel like they cannot hold a candle to them, so why pick up the pen and even try?

The Fix: Level the playing field. Mirror or support the level of drawing you are seeing at the table so far. You can always step up your own drawing when it is appropriate. Continually pass the pen and extend an invitation for others to contribute to the drawing. Step aside and invite someone else to take the marker for a while.

The Art of Reflection

Now that you know who and what to look out for, to keep your conversations from coming to a screeching halt, let's talk about proactive ways you can keep the conversation flowing. One key way to do this is to master the art of reflection.

Let's say you are visually supporting a conversation and everyone's comments and ideas are all over the place! How do you know what to reflect when you are drawing this conversation? WHAT exactly are you presenting? And how do you choose what to capture and reflect?

The key to successfully reflecting back in a visual conversation is as follows: Focus on **(1) Relevant data that is (2) correctly sorted and (3) powerfully arranged**. Let's take a closer look at each of these:

Reflections on Drawing, Data and the Brain

A few years ago I was invited to teach a brain-based "train-the-trainer" workshop for the Department of Homeland Security.[8] I was asked to use *The Art of Changing the Brain*, by James Zull, as a textbook for the course. While preparing the curriculum for this course, I found an amazing mapping that ties into how you and I draw out ideas!

James Zull is a PhD and professor of biology and biochemistry, along with serving as the director of the University Center for Innovation in Teaching and Education at Case Western Reserve University. His passion is understanding how brain research can inform teaching.

One day Zull came across the work of a psychologist named David Kolb, who was also interested in education, but was focused on something called "experiential learning." (He literally "wrote the book" about it.)[9] This grabbed Zull's attention and he started to read.

When Zull saw Kolb's model of the learning cycle, he practically fell out of his chair! Here is why:

Kolb's psychological model for learning mapped almost exactly to how Zull knew the brain received and processed information. Check it out! (I know, bear with me.)

- The sensory brain receives data, which Kolb describes as having a concrete experience of a thing.
- The brain starts to recognize and integrate disparate data into information, which Kolb describes as reflective observation.
- The brain is able to start to actually use, build upon and make meaning of the information it receives in the frontal integrative cortex, which Kolb describes as making abstract hypotheses.
- This meaning is used to determine actions in the motor cortex of the brain, which Kolb describes as active testing of the hypothesis.
- The action generates feedback, which is received as data in the sensory cortex (concrete experience) and the cycle starts all over again.

As I read this in Zull's book, I literally fell out of MY chair! Zull's brain-based learning model maps exactly onto my friend and mentor Dan Roam's four steps to visual thinking: look, see, imagine and show.[10]

- "Looking" is the receipt of data for our brains.
- "Seeing" is when we start to make sense of this data, seeing the patterns and making meaning of it so that it becomes information we can use.
- "Imagining" is creating possibilities or hypotheses based on the information we now have to work with.
- "Showing" is the testing of what we imagine to be possible, in this case by the actual drawing out of the idea.
- This action generates feedback, which we look at and the cycle starts all over again!

So, why is this so exciting to me? Because it literally proves that our brains are wired for thinking in visuals. More than this, the visual thinking process is HOW WE LEARN THINGS. For us to grow and excel—as individuals, teams or organizations—we have to learn. It just happens to work out that drawing out ideas with others is a FANTASTIC way to learn things—for us AND for them.

So, going back to my strategy for a visual conversation:

- "Look" (or in this case, "listen") for the relevant data.
- "See" the data correctly sorted for the purpose of the conversation.
- "Imagine" how you might arrange this information so the points hold power and impact for participants.
- Use drawing out the conversation as your "Show" step to generate feedback from your fellow conversationalists and start the process all over.

Because our brains are so awesome and amazing, this process takes place again and again in the blink of an eye during a conversation!

1. Relevant Data . . . WHICH Data?

A lot of ideas, information and data are discussed during a visual conversation. How do you know which data or information is relevant to your conversation's purpose? What should you reflect? There are two sides to this coin:

1. The data you want your participants to remember; and

2. The data your participants care about.

Your participants want information that will:
- Intrigue them.
- Make them smarter.
- Help them do something.
- Entertain them.
- Be easy to digest and use.
- Make them look cool!

As your group's visual conversationalist, you can share data that will:
- Educate.
- Engage.
- Be on-point to the purpose of the meeting.
- Be easy to digest and use.
- Affect behavior.
- Be worth remembering for the long term, bigger picture.

ACTIVITY: Identifying Relevant Data

- Listen to this ten-minute SoulPancake conversation between Rainn Wilson and the late, great Harold Ramis on life, art, meaning, and the power farts (yes, really!): jeannelking.com/drawforth/practice/soulpancake.[11]
- What do you think someone will want to remember from this recorded conversation? Write down the data you think is important. Don't worry about drawing it right now, just capture it in the easiest way you can while listening to this conversation.
- Look at the list you just created from listening to this conversation. Draw or sketch out the different pieces of data and information you heard you think folks would want or need to remember.
- Now listen to the talk again and draw out what you hear. Don't worry about organizing it or tying it all together, just visually make your list this time. How did this affect your choice of data to capture and reflect?

I went through this activity, too! To see what I did, and for more opportunities to practice, visit jeannelking.com /drawforth/resources.

2. Correctly Sorted . . . HOW?

We have received lots of data and information from the last exercise. But how do you start to make meaning from it and turn this data into information you can use? The first step is to start sorting it for general meaning in the following two ways:

1. Relevant and useful to your conversation's purpose; and

2. Relevant and useful to your participants

Ask yourself:
*   What are your participants interested in being able to do? Why are they having this visual conversation in the first place?

*   Which data will they need to know from you to help make this happen?

*   Which data might distract or take your visual conversation off-focus?

When listening:
*   How do you know what to focus on? How do you know what is relevant or useful? Be clear about the purpose and context for the conversation from the start and use these as your filter to shape listening.

*   Focus on what is most relevant to the purpose of your visual conversation and let go of the rest. Just because you heard something said does not mean you have to visually capture it!

ACTIVITY: Sorting the Information

*   Imagine you are going to be a visual conversationalist for a team of executives about to expand into a new market with a new widget.
*   Which types of information do you think would be the most relevant for these business owners at this time?
*   What might be confusing, overwhelming, or distracting in the information you hear that you may choose to exclude from the visual conversation?
*   What could you do with the information you hear that does not seem to be on point?

3. Powerfully Arranged...for WHAT?

At this point you have data from the conversation and you have been able to sort it into general categories to make meaning that is beneficial to the group, all remaining in alignment with the purpose of the visual conversation. Up until now, these two steps are largely mental. Now it is time to powerfully arrange this information for two different things:

1. Structure; and

2. Impact.

Ask yourself:
- What can I draw that will help provide a logical flow to the information being shared?

- Does this information build upon itself and make sense to the participants?

- Does my structure make the information easy to understand and use moving forward?

When drawing:
- Focus on clear messaging.

- Capture powerful statements.

- Make it hard to miss the point.

ACTIVITY: Powerfully Arranging

- Look back at your notes from the last two activities.
- Get your friends excited and talking about the content in the video you watched.
- How could your structural choices affect the data you share with your friends? How could you arrange your insights on the page? How would they want this information to be arranged? (Visually, of course!)

Strategize Colorfully!

Color is another fantastic tool to enhance flow, meaning and understanding of a conversation. It can be used to represent **what is said, how it is said** AND **what is not said**. Let's consider these three uses of color in your visual conversation:

What is said: Use color to organize and represent core content. Consistent use of header and sub header colors can make it easy for other folks in the conversation to track the conversation. For example, if a team's going to discuss three separate initiatives, exploring target objectives, possible challenges and possible solutions. You could color-code by initiative (different color for each one), or by desired outcome (one color for all initiative headers, but different colors for exploration topics). The choice of what to color-code depends on what you want to be able to easily track in the conversation.

How it is said: In addition to color-coding for ease or tracking, color can communicate tremendous meaning in a limited space. We are conditioned to interpret colors to mean certain things (for example, red means stop and green means go). Therefore, using colors inconsistently can confuse conversation participants. For example, if we write "GREAT!" in red, folks may get confused because red typically indicates things that are negative or needing to be stopped. Color can be a powerful way to communicate emotion.

What is not said: This can take two forms. On the one hand, there may be slight amounts of content from a long meeting or conversation, leaving you with lots of empty "white space" on your page. This abundance of white space actually says something. Consider the usefulness of letting this space stand as-is before filling it all up with decorative drawings to make the final product look pretty. It is truer to the conversation.

Color is a Tool (and a strategy)!

There is a lot of information on the psychology of color, but for our purposes we are going to turn to the psychology of color as applied to retail sales. Why retail sales? Because everybody buys stuff and because you are looking for folks to buy into this visual conversation, right?

Add your own colors to this easy-peasy guide to what colors tend to indicate to people when they view them, based again on retail sales insights:[12]

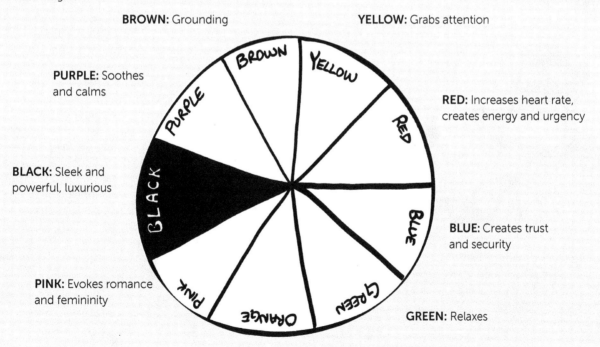

BROWN: Grounding

YELLOW: Grabs attention

PURPLE: Soothes and calms

RED: Increases heart rate, creates energy and urgency

BLACK: Sleek and powerful, luxurious

BLUE: Creates trust and security

PINK: Evokes romance and femininity

GREEN: Relaxes

ORANGE: Calls to action

How you combine these colors says something as well, so choose wisely!

> *"Your attitude is like a box of crayons that color your world.
> Constantly color your picture gray, and your picture will always be bleak.
> Try adding some bright colors to the picture by including humor,
> and your picture begins to lighten up."*
> ALLEN KLEIN

On the other hand, a person may suggest an idea, while everyone else looks down at the table and grows quiet. This quiet is taken for consensus and the person speaking moves the idea forward. In this case, what is not being said—the reaction to the idea—is just as important (if not more so) than the actual idea itself. Energy and enthusiasm can be communicated with yellows and pinks, while dampening moods can be communicated in grays and flat blue tones.

Before entering your visual conversation, have a basic color strategy for capturing and communicating core content...as well as the way it is said and what is not being said. This will make your work easier during the conversation. Participants will appreciate it when you present a consistent pattern and structure that is easy to understand, allowing for better communication and results moving forward. Now this is being of service!

Which Role Are You Playing?

Now that you are familiar with all of the ways you can keep a visual conversation flowing, what role are you going to take? Which hat are you going to wear? Are you the conversation's visual translator? Or are you an active participant in the conversation?

Although these are two distinctly different roles, both rely on the same basic skills and approach—with one significant difference. Participants add their voice to the conversation, whereas the visual translator captures the conversation but does not influence or skew the conversation.

Think of it this way. When your boss is at a meeting, it is your boss' meeting. What your boss says can carry a significant amount of weight to it.

When you wield a pen during a visual conversation—AND serve the visual translator to create the group's memory of the conversation—this effect comes into play as well. It is a slippery slope to walk upon. It is also one of the reasons why so many bosses try to facilitate their own meetings and end up failing. Instead of holding the space for folks to contribute to the conversation, the space is held (or is perceived to be held) for promoting the boss' agenda under the pretense of a conversation. This, my friend, *no es bueno!*[13]

The only way you can pull off the role of a visual translator AND a participant with any level of integrity is to only serve in one role at a time. When you wield the pen during the conversation, be of service to your group and capture the conversation. When you need to add something to the conversation, be transparent about it: ask for someone to take the marker as you shift into a participant role for the conversation. Otherwise, if you are claiming to create the group's memory of the conversation, but you are drawing what you want to add to the conversation (as opposed to what other folks are actually saying), your participants will see and recognize this, lowering the trust and integrity of their visual conversation experience.

As people see you in action, effectively navigating these two roles, they will appreciate how you are able to serve the needs of the group and contribute to the conversation in a way that maintains a high level of integrity. This is going to build trust within the group. While it will take time, eventually you may end up building a relationship with the group where they will see you are able to contribute AND accurately reflect the entire conversation at the same time!

With Great Power Comes Great Responsibility

You are the one holding the marker in this conversation (at least to start). Since you wield the marker, you may be seen as the leader of the conversation. As a visual conversationalist, you have a responsibility to be mindful of what you add to the conversation and how it is going to be received. Here are some important considerations:

- Reflect what is said, not what you think was said.
- Check your understanding of what was said with participants. Do this when you are not sure about what you heard, as well as periodically along the way.
- Receive what has been contributed and build from/upon this for your own contribution. Don't hold an idea in your pocket and listen for the opportunity to add it. Listen to the actual conversation and take part in THIS.

Now Draw Forth!

For every visual conversation, the blank page is an unexplored country with the potential to be both great and terrible. Having some simple strategies in the back of your head (or pocket) for how to approach the page can transform it into your friend and ally and facilitate your service to the group.

But how do you facilitate yourself to be of best service to the group? Ah, this is the real secret to becoming a great visual conversationalist...and it is what we are going to cover in more depth in the next section of this book.

In the meantime, here are some additional ways to help participants feel comfortable and keep the flow of visual conversation flowing!

Simple Ways to Create or Go With the Flow

- Make an intentional drawing mistake in front of the group to demonstrate you are not perfect, and they don't need to be either.
- Have folks stand with you at the board instead of sitting around a table
- If at a table, make sure there is paper on the table and markers for everyone
- When a participant shares an idea, praise and pass the pen while encouraging them to add their contribution to the group's drawing.
- Practice various color combinations and discover your favorites for visual conversations.

PART 4:
Hosting & Harvesting
Visual Conversations

How to Be in Visual Conversation

Why is it that some homes feel better than others to be in? Take my friends April and Jonny, for example. Their Craftsman home in North Park is one of my favorite places to be in the Universe.

Why is this?

I think it is because April knows how to be a Hostess with the Mostest without even trying.[1] Her home is lovely, welcoming and oh-so-comfortable. There is always a treat or a snack ready for when you show up and her two cats swing by you for some love. Whether you are sitting at the dining room table, in the comfy chairs by the fireplace, or in the made-up row of chairs and cushions for a group TV series viewing party, the conversation is always easy and you (ALWAYS) feel seen and special. When April is with you, she is WITH you.

There is a quality to being graciously and warmly hosted that is extremely attractive to be around, and this goes for hosting conversations as well. Even visual ones.

To be honest, the drawing you create during the conversation is just the tip of the iceberg everyone in the room can see. But what makes the iceberg—the visual conversation experience--so powerful is all the stuff under the water people don't see. The invitation. The comfortable space. The comfort and ease of the conversation itself.

The secret to creating and maintaining a space where people feel comfortable in conversation and great work gets done is knowing how to host yourself so you can be a good host for others.

> *"What is there more kindly than the feeling between host and guest?"*
> **AESCHYLUS**

The "Art" of Hosting a Visual Conversation

A visual conversation is not just a process: it is an artful experience. **Your real artistry emerges, not only through the images you draw, but also more importantly through how you decide to host *yourself*.** This may sound a bit counterintuitive, but just give it a moment's thought. The way you show up—and the energy you bring—to the visual conversation sets the tone for how others can show up and what they can expect from the experience. Just like any amazing conversation, hosting a visual conversation IS an experience. It is bigger than any of the words said or pictures drawn and it is powerful stuff!

Think about one of your all-time favorite experiences—perhaps it was a party, a concert, or simply standing on a mountain pass, looking at an amazing view. What do you say when people ask what it was like? "You just had to be there."

The power of experience pales beyond any words you use to describe it. This is why, for visual conversations, the most powerful experiences you create will revolve around an almost intangible quality—how you show up.

A great visual conversation does not just happen by accident. It also goes beyond merely "facilitating" a meeting or a mechanical conversation.[2] A lot of work goes into creating an experiential environment where your conversation participants can feel safe enough to engage in something meaningful and contribute their best thinking. (Especially while drawing pictures together!)

Just recently, one of my clients shared that she admires how I engage her team with ease, comfort and connection.[3] It may look like I am simply showing up and doing my thing, drawing out ideas and talking with folks. Truth is, what I am actually doing is a much deeper process. I am going to share it with you now, and it all starts with showing up.[4]

Six Essential Steps to "Showing Up":

1. **Be Present**

2. **Be Yourself**

3. **Talk About Stuff That Matters**

4. **Ask Powerful Questions**

5. **Make Space for Everyone At the Table**

6. **Reflect What You Hear**

1. Be Present: Have you ever been a part of a conversation you did not want to have end? Where the rest of the room faded away to just you and your group? The President of the United States could have walked into the room, and you guys would not even notice it because you were so tuned in and connected to what was happening in your conversation. THIS is the feeling you are going for, here! THIS is the level of engagement and presence. Not just for the conversation, but for yourself as well.

2. Be Yourself: Show up free from the roles and assumptions that follow you. Sometimes when we have a conversation, we are not actually speaking with people... even though we really want to. Instead, we are speaking with the "role" this person holds. When we do this, we limit what we bring to a conversation and block ideas. Know what I mean?

Every single one of us has roles we show up in, in work and in life. Whether you are a business owner, employee, father, mother, daughter, brother, wife, husband, boyfriend, girlfriend, friend, coworker, or CEO—or any combination thereafter—each role comes with different assumptions, perspectives and reality. As such, your responses and how you show up can vary accordingly.[5] By stepping out of your "role" and speaking from your core/heart, possibilities show up that never would be given the chance to join in the conversation otherwise.

3. Talk About Stuff That Matters: Focus on talking about stuff that touches people and can make a difference, even if there is no easy answer. Especially when there is no easy answer! It is in these very situations that conversation becomes more important than any sort of formal problem-solving process. The best conversations are ones that invite you to dig in and contribute your best thinking and ideas. Not the ones where you stand around on the sidelines, nodding and saying, "Yep!" Host conversations that give people a chance to take on the things that really matter to them and possibly even make a positive contribution to their solution.

4. Ask Powerful Questions: Powerful questions challenge the way you think about things and open up possibilities. Remember, the good stuff grows when you dig in. How satisfying is your role in a conversation when all you are doing is saying "yes" and "no" to someone else's questions? Open-ended questions invite folks to share their thoughts and make for way more interesting conversation! Plus, a well-crafted question can create a fundamental shift in the way you perceive challenges, engage with others and take action.[6]

5. Make Space for Everyone at the Table: When you talk with people who think exactly like you it is not really the type of conversation we are looking for, because the ideas are all pretty much the same. It is when people hold different thoughts and views from ours that the conversation starts to get really juicy! Instead of keeping these folks out of the conversation, invite them in and make sure they feel like they have got a place at the table to pull up a chair and dig into the topic at hand.[7] This leads to working partnerships that blend new levels of knowledge, experience and practice. Having the right people at the table for your conversation can create and maintain the space for diverse voices to feel comfortable and welcome to join in.

6. Reflect What You Hear: As we have discussed before (and I cannot stress this enough), it is important for people to feel seen, heard and understood. Part of this is mirroring back what you hear in conversation to check for understanding, but the biggest way we reflect back is through drawing our visual conversations. This interactive process supports the group's learning and creativity and helps build a shared commitment to action.[8]

Jeannel's "Secret Sauce" for Hosting

Just as my friend April has developed a uniquely welcoming way to host people in her home, I have learned to develop my own "secret sauce" of sorts, for hosting visual conversations. Looking at my own practice, I do a lot of up-front work—with others and with myself—to create and maintain the space for a great conversation to occur. After all, if I cannot host myself, I cannot host others. I also believe in practicing what I preach. As such this "secret sauce" essentially boils down to three ingredients:[9]

1. Host Yourself

- Create and maintain an internal space for yourself where you can stay fully present to the needs and experiences of the group.

- Prepare for the conversation and then let this preparation go so you can be fully present to the actual conversation.

2. Host the Conversation

- Clarify the "true purpose" of the conversation at hand and ensure the conversation and questions are in alignment with this purpose.

- Be transparent in role and purpose and in service to your group.

3. Host the Community

- Extend an invitation to everyone who should have a seat at the table for this conversation

- Create a welcoming, enticing, and safe environment that people will want to come to and engage in a conversation that matters.

- Engage everyone in the process so insights are co-created, outcomes are co-owned and people are 100% informed and vested in making these outcomes a reality.

The way we show up is how everyone around us gets to show up. Your ability to host the needs of the conversation and the participants is in direct relationship to your ability to host yourself. Only by being fully present to what you bring to the table, can you fully support others to do the same. It is the foundation on which everything else is built. The best thing you can do is take good care of this foundation!

ACTIVITY: Taking Care of Your Foundation

In the space below, draw a picture of yourself ready to be fully present to the conversation and to those around you.

What do you look like when you show up this way? How do you feel? What do you need to do to ensure that you can show up in this way for yourself and for others? Take a moment and note your thoughts in with your picture.

> *"Don't be afraid to give up the good to go for the great."*
> JOHN D. ROCKEFELLER

Four Keys to Go From Good to GREAT

There are four requirements that come into play when you focus on making just "good" visual conversations into GREAT ones. I have put the rubber to the road on all of these and have learned that **all four need to be in place for the magic to happen: (1) Show Up, (2) Participate, (3) Contribute, and (4) Connect.**[10]

1. Show Up

Showing up is foundational to any visual conversation. A GREAT visual conversation relies on the ability to create and maintain a space where participants can be fully present to the conversation, instead of being distracted by where they would rather be or what they would rather be doing. Being present to the conversation starts with YOU. When you show up fully to the conversation, you encourage and support others to be fully present in the visual conversation as well.

How to do it: Start by checking any excess mental and/or emotional baggage at the door before entering the visual conversation. You can always pick it back up and take it with you on the way out. But it cannot go inside the room with you: it needs to stay outside so you can be fully present to the conversation. Otherwise, you will just be tired and distracted, which will make everyone else tired and distracted.[11] When you are fully present, it makes it easier for your participants to be fully present with you.

Checking baggage at the door is no easy task. Try meditating, breathe work, or create setting-up rituals to strip away any of the "stuff", until your mind is as clear and ready as the white page you brought to capture the conversation. Believe me: the more you practice this, the easier it will become.

Draw Forth & Journal: How do you currently show up to conversations? What does the meeting space feel like when your team gets together? How present are the people in the room to the conversation? What changes can you make to give your team permission to be more present during conversations? How else could you give yourself permission to be more present?

2. Participate

Participation fosters listening, suspends judgments and biases and exposes these biases when they pop up to promote more honest communication. By fully participating in the conversation, you can activate other concentric circles to do so as well.

Draw Forth & Journal: What could it look like to participate fully in a conversation? What might keep you from participating fully? What assumptions do you bring to the table when you engage in conversation with your team? Consider assumptions about your team members, about the subject matter of the conversation or the work you do. What elephants live in the room? Which cows are too sacred to be touched? Which snakes are hiding in the grass? How do these assumptions affect the conversations you have? How can you host these assumptions to show up in a more visible way, so they can be addressed or simply acknowledged during your next conversation?

How to do it: Become aware of the "usual" judgments and assumptions you bring to conversations, and "call them out" when you notice them rising up within you. Focus on breathing the conversation and paying attention to whether or not you are responding to something or "reacting" to it. Reactions are typically indicators you are acting upon a judgment or assumption.

To "call out" judgments and assumptions from others, focus on identifying the snakes lurking in the grass just waiting to bite, or the elephant in the room everyone is dancing around, or the sacred cow nobody seems willing to touch. Make friends with the snakes, elephants and cows.[12] You can also share a reflection with the rest of the group that "it seems as if we are dancing around this elephant," and check in with them to see if they are experiencing this as well. Usually, someone else is. Typically, many others are.

3. Contribute

Contribution can show up in a visual conversation in four ways. You can: (1) contribute your best thinking and the connections you see to the conversation, (2) contribute your voice and ideas to the mix, (3) contribute your marker to help harvest and capture the insights (and other "good stuff") from the conversation, and (4) contribute your presence to witness the conversation. Your skill set is a gift to yourself and others. When you use your gifts in service to others, you contribute to making great things possible for everyone involved.

How to do it: Share what you need to while also actively inviting others to join in the fun on all four of these levels (thinking, voice, drawings and presence). Be sensitive to people in the conversation who choose to contribute by simply bearing witness to it, or who prefer to listen for the majority of the time, and drop a bombshell of insight into the conversation towards the end.

Draw Forth & Journal: How do you typically contribute to a conversation? How do people close to you tend to contribute? How does this knowledge affect how you might show up for your next conversation? What can you do to help everyone share their thinking, voice and drawings in a visual conversation?

4. Connect

Visual conversations make ideas visible. Visual conversations also require vulnerability, because there is nothing to hide behind: everyone is sharing ideas that are being reflected onto the drawing surface in real time. In order to share deeply amongst the group, a certain level of trust and rapport must be built.[13] Connecting with each other in ideas and in conversation allows us to accomplish this.

How to do it: Listen for larger patterns in the conversation. When these patterns emerge, make the connections on paper and share what you are hearing/seeing with the rest of the people in the conversation. Get a reality check from the rest of the group and see if they are experiencing the same thing.

Draw Forth & Journal: Who have you always wanted to have a conversation with in your community? What could it look like to invite them to a visual conversation over a shared interest?

Walking the Line: Providing "Just Enough" Structure

What happens when you try to control or provide too many rules or structure around a conversation? It stops being juicy and fun, right? It stifles the flow of ideas and creativity. Yet at the same time, structure is helpful to keep a conversation from turning into a free-for-all shouting match where nobody hears a thing anyone else is saying.

As a visual conversationalist, you will walk a fine line between representing order and control that (if not checked) stifles creativity and the juicy chaos of creative insights and conversation. Visa Card inventor Dee Hock named the space between chaos and order the Chaordic field.[14] I know! It is a crazy name! But this field between chaos and order is the space in which you will work and host conversations. In other words, as a visual conversationalist, you have to keep a foot in both worlds. [15]

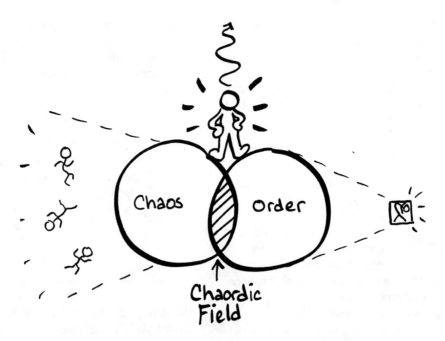

Chaos

Order

Chaordic Field

With one foot, you need to embrace the chaos and draw out ideas with people, turning conversations into works of art! (So to speak!) And during this process, anything goes! Yet with the other foot, you need to bring just enough structure and organization to the conversation visualization so it is helpful and meaningful to the group. This also ensures people don't get lost in the drawing and you don't lose track of what is being discussed.

If you drew whatever you wanted, however you wanted to draw it, then other folks might be completely lost and confused looking at what you are creating while they speak. Your job is to hold the visual space open enough so ideas and conversation are invited to flow freely, while at the same time providing just enough order and structure to your drawing so it makes sense to—and can be used well by—the group having the conversation. Since conversations are living, breathing things, its need for chaos and order varies as well.

When the conversation shuts down, it can be a sign that things have become too rigid. This is your cue to introduce a bit more chaos to the process. To open things up. When things seem all over the place, this is your cue to introduce a bit more structure to help shape and guide the conversation.

When engaging in juicy conversations about things that don't have clear-cut answers or solutions, it is possible to become lost in the chaos that may arise. (If you have ever looked at a spirited online forum thread, you know what I mean! That discussion thread can go all sorts of places!) It is also possible that people may choose to impose order on the process, perhaps even to control the process or dictate its outcome. (Hello...online forum again!)

By using your visual conversations to ask powerful questions that matter, you introduce an element of chaos into an otherwise-ordered existence. To keep the conversation from becoming too chaotic, and people from feeling too frustrated and powerless from not having cut-and-dried answers to the questions they are exploring, you can introduce visual forms to shape and contain the discussion (your conversation shapers). As you walk this ever-changing line between too much order and chaos in a conversation, you help our folks work through fear and confusion in ways that encourage the emergence of new thinking and innovation.

> *"The problem is never how to get new, innovative thoughts into your mind, but how to get old ones out."*
> DEE HOCK

Now Draw Forth!

By now, you have probably picked up on the fact that physical tools and drawing skills are just the tip of the iceberg for serving as a visual conversationalist. When it comes to drawing conversations with others that draw forth the best in our work and ourselves, *how* we show up to these conversations makes all the difference.

How might you practice and further refine your ability to host yourself so you can skillfully host others in visual conversation? Here are some additional tips to help you BE in visual conversation:

Draw Forth & BE in Conversation

- **Be present: model it for and with others to help them be more present as well.**
- **Join like-minded people to join them in visual conversation.**
- **Play with the power of your questions. How well do your questions cut to the heart of the inquiry?**
- **Practice just listening. What do you hear with your ears? With your eyes? With your heart? Can you let go of needing to add to (or interrupt, or commandeer) the conversation and simply be a witness to it?**
- **How can you help yourself others engage in listening well? Establishing conversation etiquette or guidelines up front? Use of a talking piece? Experiment with ways that work for your particular needs.**

9

Living, Breathing, Visual Conversations

Visual conversations are alive: living, breathing experiences. In order to truly understand this, let's take a moment to take a breath together.

Start by sitting in a relaxed position, with your feet on the floor.

Now, take a slow, deep breath in.

Then, slowly allow all of your breath to exhale....

Go through this breathing cycle again. As you take another deep breath in, see if you notice that pause at the top before you exhale.

Did you notice it?

This same in-breath, pause, out-breath flow happens in conversation as well. A great conversation—one that comes alive, pulling you in to do great work and get great results—actually unfolds in a pattern similar to breathing. Understanding the pattern or breath of your conversations will better prepare you to visualize, participate and host within them.

If you compare breathing to a conversation flow, the in-breath is where you do your divergent thinking, then there is the holding spot where things may get a little uncomfortable, and then the out-breath becomes your conversation's convergence. Sam Kaner calls this pattern the Diamond of Participation:[1]

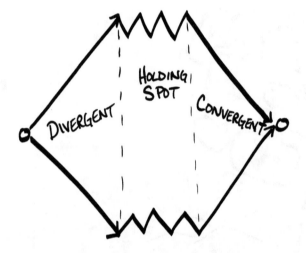

What do I mean when I say "divergent thinking?" This is when you really dive into a topic, exploring every facet and possibility and start generating ideas.

Divergent Thinking Shows Up in the Following Ways

- **Generating alternatives**
- **Free-for-all open discussion**
- **Gathering diverse points of view**
- **Unpacking the logic of a problem**

My friends and I have a standing "Dinner-and-a-TV Series Episode" gathering every Sunday. After we watch our favorite show's most recent episode, we have a conversation about it. The conversation always seems to start with: "Oh my gosh! What did you think of THAT?!" And we start tossing topics out all over the place! I remember when my friends and I gathered to watch the season seven mid-series finale for Mad Men. When the episode ended, our conversation started and it was all OVER the place:

what is going to happen to Don Draper, what is going to happen with the agency, what is Peggy going to do when she realizes Ted is going to be back in town? And this was just the start of it—we were covering more ideas and topics by the minute! This is what I mean by divergent thinking.

Alternatively, convergent thinking is when everyone comes together and discusses the same topic. Instead of each of us tossing out Mad Men observations, a few of us might start to lock in on how Roger needed to tell Burt to BECOME a leader. Whereas others might converge on how Don and Peggy were becoming an amazing, heart-touching team. Before you know it we would all be talking about how these two factors might shape the fate of the agency in the last seven episodes of the season.

Convergent Thinking Shows Up in the Following Ways

- **Evaluating alternatives**
- **Summarizing key points**
- **Sorting ideas into categories**
- **Arriving at general conclusions.**

In between these is a space containing the struggle to move from divergent thinking into convergent thinking. This "holding of one's breath" space, the space before the exhale, is called the "Groan Zone."[2] It is one of the more difficult and uncomfortable places to be (and stay) in during a conversation. It is also a VITAL component of a powerful conversation.

This is where ideas compete against each other. This is where compromises have to be made for the group to move forward. In the convergent phase of a conversation, I could talk all I wanted about what Peggy would do once she realized Ted was back in town. But to move forward with the conversation, all of our competing interests would need to get resolved. Not just resolved, but HONORED and resolved.

Ever been in a conversation where you are talking about something and the person you are talking with keeps saying the same thing from ten minutes ago? Do you get a bit frustrated when this happens? Like they are not really a part of the conversation? Only pursuing their own agenda? This often happens because the person speaking never really felt heard, so they are not ready to move on with the conversation.[3] When we feel this way, it can be oh so tempting to simply bail on the conversation. Especially when we are stuck in the Groan Zone!

How to Keep Them In

By being aware of the breath of a conversation, you can identify when folks are generating ideas and support this visually by drawing these ideas out. Then, when you move into the Groan Zone of the conversation, you have all of these ideas captured so nobody needs to keep bringing one up to make sure it was heard—it is clear it was heard

because you have got it on the sheet. So now you can start to evaluate what you have got and make some informed decisions. Sure, ideas will compete: this is part of the Groan Zone, too! But at some point—and this almost ALWAYS happens—someone will say something, there will be good-natured laughter and the pressure bubble of the Groan Zone will pop. People will then easily identify the few ideas they want to chew on. The results of this conversation will often set the stage for what we talk about next.

And so the breathing pattern starts over once more, just in time for my Sunday dinner group to have dessert![4]

ACTIVITY: Finding Your Groan Zone

In the space below, draw out your own Diamond of Participation. Next, think about the last conversation you were in that really mattered to you. See how this conversation maps onto the diamond: where did ideas grow and expand, where did things get a bit challenging or difficult, and how did the conversation resolve? Take a few moments to draw out your insights and reflections on how understanding this patter can influence your engagement in visual conversations moving forward.

Harvesting Conversations – Easy As Apple Pie

So far, you have had a juicy and productive conversation with folks and you have drawn out what has been discussed. But there is a difference between visually capturing the content of a conversation and HARVESTING the yummy goodness of this conversation. Your drawing represents the conversation. Harvesting promotes understanding and is where learning and growth occurs in the conversation process. Your visuals are a key part of this harvesting process.

Your visual conversations help people discover and work with the convergent aspects of their conversation without losing a thing. When you draw forth these conversation insights, you weave different strands of the conversation together into new and useful forms. You create something more from them than there was in the original conversation.

Take a moment to visualize a pile of apples. The drawings you create during a conversation may be all the apples you collect. Here is an apple. There is an apple. Here is another one! Yep, you have got lots of apples!

When you harvest the fruit of your conversation, however, you know more than the fact that you have got a bushel of apples. You also know what you can do with them! (Hey, we have enough apples for a pie! Let's make one! Hey, this is going to be a lot of pie...what should we do with it?)

Looks like you have got the seed for your next round of conversation!

> *"You must give to get, You must sow the seed, before you can reap the harvest."*
> SCOTT REED

The Merry Harvesters

I don't remember the first time I made an apple pie, but I do remember my first experience intentionally harvesting a discussion!

In 2007, I attended my first Art of Hosting gathering (this is fancy speak for a facilitation experiential-learning retreat).[7] On the first day, a man with ruggedly handsome features, long hair and a super-cool hat stood up and introduced the idea of harvesting. Rather than lose what we were learning, this guy named Chris Corrigan explained there would be a team of people—"Merry Harvesters"—who would take on the responsibility of collecting the insights from various group conversations, distill and synthesize them into the essence of the learning, then reflect them back to the group in interesting and creative ways.[8] I envisioned people prancing about in tights and medieval garb, dancing through the forest and singing tales of the lessons learned throughout our retreat. So, of course, I raised my hand and volunteered.

It was one of the most important volunteer moments of my life.

After all, I had grown pretty comfortable with harvesting ideas for myself and I was even okay doing it in front of my team. But deep in my heart of hearts, I never really did it FOR my team. If I am honest with myself, these visual harvests I created during my company's meetings and conversations were more for myself than anyone else: I enjoyed doing them, and other people just happened to benefit.

So this was a big shift for me – going from harvesting to please and make sense for myself, to harvesting in service of a larger group. Thank goodness I volunteered, because this single shift—moving from drawing to serve myself to drawing to serve others— became a cornerstone for my practice as a facilitator and a foundation for my business to this day.

When you harvest your visual conversation, you gather and distill the big ideas and core content so it can be fed back into the system and serve as a launching point for the next conversation. (I did quite a bit of research on this topic for my master's thesis on the Art of Hosting organizations and conversations!)[5] Just as seeds contain stored energy for a plant to grow, so does the harvest of your visual conversation. The visual harvest you create contains aspects of the group's energy and process. When participants revisit their visual conversation images, they tap back into the energy of these original conversations and become reinvigorated to make these discussed outcomes a reality.[6]

A Peek Inside Jeannel's Head for How to Harvest

Sometimes a conversation is easy-peasy. Other times it is more complex and the group outcome really matters. The process of supporting conversations like these start WAY before the conversation itself even does, and goes well beyond the end of the conversation. When approached with a more complex meeting, I approach the conversation with a bigger-picture strategy, and it all goes back to what I learned while prancing about in tights as a Merry Harvester with Chris Corrigan all those years ago.[9]

1. Clarify the Purpose: It is essential to get crystal clear up front on the purpose of the conversation. Not what participants "say" the purpose is, but what the true purpose is for the conversation.[10] (Have you ever been invited to something only to discover that it was under false pretense and they really wanted to talk about something else? Yeah, this is what we want to avoid here!)

Draw Forth Outcome: Clarify the purpose for the conversation, a set of questions about this purpose, a pre-determined place to use the result of the harvest and specific tools to use in doing our work.

2. Prepare Yourself: Revisiting our three concentric circles from chapter 8, start with you. Clear your mind of any distractions or competing interests and become a blank slate to reflect the conversation back to the group. Prepare yourself as host, embodying the spirit of the invitation and setting the context for the conversation.

"How can people trust the harvest, unless they see it sown?"
MARY RENAULT

Draw Forth Outcome: Setting the tone for the process to come, a level of seriousness and depth (and fun!) being communicated about the process.

Draw Forth Outcome: Conversation, exploration, safety, trust, insights, results, laughter and fellowship.

3. *Plan for the Future:* At one level, there is the conversation you are about to have. On another level, there is the change you want the conversation to make or effect you want the conversation to have for the future. Lock in on what this future desired outcome is, and—using a bit of my "Back to the Future" approach from Chapter 5—reverse engineer what had to happen during your upcoming conversation for this future state or objective to have been achieved. Who needed to benefit from it? How did the harvest best serve or add value to achieving this future outcome? What form was most effective for our visual conversation to take?

6. *Harvest Insights and Pass The Basket:* Visually capture and reflect core content and key ideas of the conversation as they emerge, so participants know what their core conversational fruits are as you go along. It is important to pass the pen and invite others to capture what they hear emerging from the conversation so it is not just "your" representation of what happened: it is everyone's.

Draw Forth Outcome: A clear purpose and success criteria for the visual conversation and its harvest.

Draw Forth Outcome: Creation of a collaborative record or collective memory of the conversation.

4. *Pack a Pocketful of Seeds:* Think of possible seed questions and visual conversation shapers to support and structure the conversation at the right time and in the right conditions for the process. Then, put these seeds and shapers into your proverbial back pocket and promptly forget them!

7. *Prepare and Process the Fruit:* Take the resulting drawings from the visual conversation and digitally scan them into files that are easily shared with participants. Sharing the digital results with the rest of the group as quickly as possible to retain their content's "freshness."

Draw Forth Outcome: A basic idea of ways you may approach your visual conversation and a back-up "emergency kit" of questions and shapers, should you need them.

Draw Forth Outcome: Continued engagement, ownership and easy sharing of the results of the conversation by its participants.

8. *Feed it Forward:* Use the resulting images to generate new questions and clarify a shared understanding with the group. Identify next steps and low-hanging fruit to take action upon.

5. *Tend Your Field:* Everything contributes to people's experience of a conversation.[11] Create and maintain the space for people to engage in a powerful conversa-tion—from the way you show up, draw and interact with people in conversation, to the way you dress. This allows participants to relax into the conversation, feel safe and comfortable and go deeper, faster than they ever expected.

Draw Forth Outcome: Better decisions, targeted actions and valued results.

ACTIVITY: Harvest Your Own Insights

Now it is time for you to create your own plan for harvesting visual conversations! How do you want to show up for these conversations? What will you want to have when you walk into the room? How will you choose to be? What "seeds" will you want in your back pocket, just in case you need them? And how will you pass the pen so others may join in the fun? Take a few moments and draw your insights in the space below.

Now Draw Forth!

When you take a deep breath to begin a conversation, the conversation takes a deep breath, too. Knowing this helps you navigate the flow of a conversation and be present to all stages of the conversation's process.

By being present to what is, and to what is emerging, you encourage and support others to be fully present in the conversation. As the conversation progresses, you rely upon various listening tools, including your ears, heart, or use of a talking piece to preserve the space for deep attention and listening to occur.

You harvest the wisdom, shared learning, and co-creation that emerges from the conversation so the conversation has lasting value for the group or community. Once the harvest has been collected and understood, clarity emerges, the right decisions can be made and wise action can be taken.

So now you have got the tools, framework, strategy, mindset and the Art for hosting visual conversations—it is time to truly Draw Forth!

Some Last Tips for Harvesting Visual Conversations

- **Pay attention to the conversations you take part in. Be aware of when you are in a divergent phase, convergent phase, or if you are sitting in the Groan Zone. Notice how the conversation is different in each of these phases.**
- **Listen for the seeds in your conversations. What ideas or insights want to be built on or explored for the next round of conversation?**
- **It is easy for people to tell when we say we want to talk about one thing, but we really want to talk about something else. If you are unclear about the purpose of a conversation, reflect it back to the group for a reality check.**
- **Make clearing your mind a regular practice. My go-to practices for clearing my mind include meditating, listening to music, and taking a few conscious breaths. Explore different processes and see which ones work best for you!**
- **Before harvesting a visual conversation, ask how things will be different as a result of us having had this conversation. Then, harvest for this outcome instead of for the conversation itself.**
- **Don't let your preparations prevent you from being fully present to what happens in the conversation. Prepare prior to the conversation, and let it all go when you show up for the conversation. Trust that your prep work will pop back up in your brain when it is appropriate for it to do so.**
- **Remember: the way we show up is how everyone else gets to show up! Show up ready to engage in and harvest an amazing conversation, and others will do the same.**

Drawing Forth

When we started this journey together, we were chatting about alchemy and the possibilities of drawing conversations with other people. And now look at you—you are on track to start conjuring up a bit of alchemy of your own! At this point you have:

- A basic tool kit for engaging in visual conversations.

- A visual language to help you effectively communicate during these conversations.

- Conversation shapers for shaping visual conversations.

- An awesome Good Enough mindset for drawing out ideas with others, including making best (or at least better) friends with your inner critics and giving yourself permission to pick up the pen and play with drawing out ideas.

- Strategies and insights for approaching and working the blank page during visual conversations.

- An appreciation and understanding of the art of hosting and harvesting these living, breathing, visual conversations.

But what happens when you put this book down and move on with your life? Just like when we learned a second language in school, will you continue to practice and grow your skills? Or will you set it aside, not use it and lose the skills you have built so far?

My hope is that you are ready to keep growing and cultivating these visual conversationalist skills within yourself and for others. You already know this language; all you need now is to get comfortable visually conversing with others. This is just a matter of practice, and not just with a pen.

Visual conversations are—at their essence—a personal practice: when you "show up" and host yourself, you become able to create and hold the space for others to "show up" and host themselves. When we draw out ideas together in this way, we end up drawing forth the best in ourselves and in each other. This is where the magic of a visual conversation truly lies: not in revamping a process, but in bringing depth to family, organizational or team experience and understanding by committing to host yourself as an individual.

And what a host you will be! You now have all the tools and knowledge you need to be a successful visual conversationalist. Don't judge yourself against standards you would not use on others. We are quick to find the beauty in others' drawings and sometimes just focus on the things we don't like about our own, so remember to see the good in your work.

If you run into roadblocks, contact me. If you want to show me what you created, contact me.

You are Good Enough to do this. Your drawings are Good Enough, and you are Good Enough. You are worthy of being seen and heard in this world. The world needs your drawings. The world needs your voice. The world needs your visual conversations. But most of all, the world needs you to show up as fully and authentically as you possibly can, as often as you can. The only thing left to do is to pick up the pen, get out into the world and actually do it!

I cannot wait to see what you draw forth!

Jeannel

A Few of My Favorite Things
(Resources)

Things to know before you explore:

I use what I recommend. All the resources listed here are ones I personally use and like. No blind recommendations or paid endorsements here!

I'm a Mac user. As a result, there aren't many resources listed for Windows/PC users. (Sorry!)

I love paper. Books, in particular. Maybe it is the GenX coming out in me, or maybe it is because I have always been an avid reader. So while there are websites listed here, don't discount the books. (Because they rock!)

I believe that what you draw is Good Enough. You won't find any master-class drawing resources here. If what you draw is Good Enough to get your ideas across in real-time, then what you draw is Good Enough for this!

What works for me may not work for you. We are different people with different needs, after all. Feel free to use what works for you and leave what doesn't. I won't be offended!

I believe there's always more out there. Got a great resource that is not on the list? Tell me about it; I am always looking to learn and grow!

Brain Science

The Art of Changing the Brain: Enriching the Practice of Teaching by Exploring the Biology of Learning, by James E. Zull

Brain Rules: 12 Principles for Surviving and Thriving at Work, Home, and School, by John Medina

The Creative Brain, by Ned Herrmann

A Whole New Mind: Why Right-Brainers Will Rule the Future, by Daniel Pink

Zen and the Brain: Toward an Understanding of Meditation and Consciousness, by James H. Austin

Conversations

The Art of Convening: Authentic Engagement in Meetings, Gatherings, and Conversations, by Craig & Patricia Neal, with Cynthia Wold

The Art of Powerful Questions: Catalyzing Insight, Innovation, and Action, by Eric Vogt, Juanita Brown, and David Isaacs.

The Circle Way: A Leader in Every Chair, by Christina Baldwin.

SoulPancake: Chew on Life's Big Questions, by Rainn Wilson.

The World Café: Shaping Our Futures Through Conversations That Matter, by Juanita Brown, David Isaacs, World Cafe Community and Peter Senge.

Hosting Yourself & Others

Art of Hosting website:
www.artofhosting.com

Awake At Work: 35 Practical Buddhist Principles for Discovering Clarity and Balance in the Midst of Work's Chaos, by Michael Carroll

Be Our Guest: Perfecting the Art of Customer Service, by The Disney Institute and Theodore Kinni

Chris Corrigan's website:
www.chriscorrigan.com

Let Your Life Speak: Listening for the Voice of Vocation, by Parker J. Palmer

Sabbath: Finding Rest, Renewal, and Delight In Our Busy Lives, by Wayne Muller

Start with Why: How Great Leaders Inspire Everyone to Take Action, by Simon Sinek

World Cafe website:
www.theworldcafe.com

Mindset

Awakening the Giant Within, by Anthony Robbins

Choosing Me Before We, by Christine Arylo

Creating: A practical guide to the creative process and how to use it to create anything - a work of art, a relationship, a career or a better life, by Robert Fritz

Feel the Fear . . . And Do It Anyway, by Susan Jeffers, Ph.D.

Make Your Creative Dreams Real: A Plan for Procrastinators, Perfectionists, Busy People, and People Who Would Really Rather Sleep All Day, by SARK

Mastery: The Keys to Success and Long-Term Fulfillment, by George Leonard

Permission: A Guide to Generating More Ideas, Being More of Yourself and Having More Fun at Work, by Pamela Meyer and Brandy Agerbeck

What You Draw is Good Enough, by Jeannel King

Strategy & Approach

The Facilitator's Guide to Participatory Decision Making, by Sam Kaner et al.

The Fifth Discipline Fieldbook: Strategies and Tools for Building a Learning Organization, by Peter M. Senge

The Graphic Facilitator's Guide: How to use your listening, thinking and drawing skills to make meaning, by Brandy Agerbeck

Rapid Problem-Solving With Post-It Notes, by David Straker

The Sketchnote Handbook: the illustrated guide to visual note taking, by Mike Rohde

Visual Meetings: How Graphics, Sticky Notes and Idea Mapping Can Transform Group Productivity, by David Sibbet

Thinkertoys: A Handbook of Creative-Thinking Techniques (2nd Edition), by Michael Michalko

Understanding Comics: The Invisible Art, by Scott McCloud

Supplies & Materials

Artist & Craftsman Supply, for general art supplies. US Locations and an on-line store: www.artistcraftsman.com

Dick Blick Art Supply, for general art supplies. U.S. Locations and an online store: www.dickblick.com

Drawing Apps, for inexpensive drawing apps for your tablet: visit your iTunes app store or Android app store online

Michael's, for general art supplies. U.S. & Canada locations and an online store: www.michaels.com.

Neuland, for facilitation supplies and nontoxic refillable markers. Germany locations and an online store: www.neuland.com

PanPastel® artist's pastels: www.panpastel.com

Stattys, for static-cling sticky notes: www.statys.com

Zuca® Bag, for travel-friendly gear storage: www.zuca.com

Visual Language

The Back of the Napkin: Solving Problems and Selling Ideas with Pictures, by Dan Roam

Beyond Words: A Guide to Drawing Out Ideas, by Milly Sonneman

Discovery Doodles: Sketchbook Basics, by Alicia Diane Durand

Google Images, for an online icon dictionary and thesaurus: www.images.google.com

The Grimace Project, for an interactive resource to understand how to compose facial expressions: www.grimace-project.net

How to Draw a Good Enough... online drawing tutorials: www.jeannelking.com/goodenough

Make A World, by Ed Emberley

The Noun Project, for an online icon dictionary: www.thenounproject.com

Visual Thinking: Tools for Mapping Your Ideas, by Nancy Margulies and Christine Valenza

Yossarian, for a searchable online metaphor engine: www.yossarianlives.com

Visual Templates & Other Conversation Shapers

Bikablo® Visual Dictionary: www.bikablo.com/produkte

Business Model Generation: A Handbook for Visionaries, Game Changers, and Challengers, by Alexander Osterwalder and Yves Pigneur

Digital Graphic Guides, from Grove Consultants International: www.grove.com

The Doodle Revolution: Unlock the Power to Think Differently, by Sunni Brown

Drawing Solutions: How Visual Goal Setting Will Change Your Life, by Patti Dobrowolski

Gamestorming: A Playbook for Innovators, Rulebreakers, and Changemakers, by Dave Gray, Sunni Brown, & James Macanufo

The Mind Map Book: How to Use Radiant Thinking to Maximize Your Brain's Untapped Potential, by Tony Buzan with Barry Buzan

Napkin Academy: www.napkinacademy.com

Up Your Creative Genius: www.upyourcreativegenius.com

Notes

CHAPTER 1

1. For a deep-dive into why this is the case, read *The Doodle Revolution: Unlock the Power to Think Differently*, by my friend and colleague, Sunni Brown. For a quick overview on this topic, check out her TED talk as well at http://www.ted.com/talks/sunni_brown?language=en. Good stuff!

2. "Learning in a Visual Age: The Critical Importance of Visual Arts Education, by the National Art Education Association: http://www.arteducators.org/learning/learning-in-a-visual-age/NAEA_LVA_09.pdf.

3. These visual conversations have been so successful that other Special Forces units have followed suit! Each one of these projects blows my mind and reframes my beliefs around who could be open to hosting visual conversations.

4. Let's hear it for online dictionaries! http://www.oxforddictionaries.com/us/definition/american_english/conversation

5. http://www.oxforddictionaries.com/us/definition/american_english/idea

6. http://www.oxforddictionaries.com/us/definition/american_english/conversation

7. http://www.oxforddictionaries.com/us/definition/american_english-thesaurus/conversation

8. Really! It's okay! There are no wrong or right answers, here. There is only what you see in these drawings. Whatever jumps out at you is awesome.

CHAPTER 2

1. I was certainly nervous when someone asked me to draw a conversation for the first time (as an adult)! You can read about how my nerves got the best of me, and what happened, in the next section (The "Jackass" Myth).

2. http://www.statisticbrain.com/fear-phobia-statistics/

3. I'm kidding. Of COURSE it's scary! It's something new! But you can totally do this, so keep on reading.

4. Yes, it's capitalized. And you will see "Good Enough" in caps throughout this book. This is intentional. It is the proper name of a specific concept—and core tenet—of my business practice and philosophy. To learn more, read my eBook, <u>What You Draw Is Good Enough</u>, or visit www.jeannelking.com/blog/goodenough.

5. http://dictionary.reference.com/browse/fear

6. This has never actually happened to me, but it doesn't stop me from worrying about it!

7. Milarepa is generally considered to be one of Tibetan Buddhism's most famous yogis. I've adapted this particular story from Tricycle Magazine: http://www.auraglaser.com/wp-content/uploads/2012/09/Spring12Tricycle.AuraGlaser.pdf

8. Thanks to Susan Jeffers, Ph.D., for introducing this concept into the mainstream with her classic self-help book, *Feel The Fear . . . And Do It Anyway*.

9. This was only because I was physically unable to do anything else at the time! My dominant arm had to become literally disabled for me to pick up the marker and start drawing out my own ideas. Don't wait for your own work injury: pick up the pen and have fun now!

10. http://en.wikipedia.org/wiki/Inner_critic

11. Psychologists Earley and Weiss, for example, identified seven basic types of inner critics: the Perfectionist, the Taskmaster, the Inner Controller, the Guilt Tripper, the Destroyer, the Underminer, and the Molder. I was introduced to my particular inner critics while attending the Inner Mean Girl Reform School with Christine Arylo and Amy Ahlers.

12. My perfectionist inner critic, for example, knows that I could do really great work if I put my mind to it. She wants me to do well, and she helps me adhere to high standards. Sometimes, though, those high standards can get really high! When this happens, she's no longer helping me but hindering my ability—and willingness—to aim high.

13. Smartass. (I adore my dad!)

CHAPTER 3

1. I have put this one to the test, believe me! During a whiteboard animation shoot, my client wanted an object to look shiny-silver on the video. Of course, none of the gray dry erase markers gave the same effect. So we busted out the silver permanent markers and I laid the ink down thick to get the effect the client wanted. It took quite a few dry erase markers to do it, but with some persistence and quite a bit of elbow grease it all got erased and we continued on with the shoot. (Hint: if you ever are asked to use a permanent marker on a whiteboard animation shoot, do yourself a favor and shoot that portion last!)

2. For purchasing information, see the Resources section.

3. When it comes to digital drawing, layers are where the magic happens. You can create one layer for your background, another layer for your image, another layer below that for some shading effects, another layer for text, et cetera. With each layer, you can move them, resize them, change them out, and delete them all without having to recreate your drawing from scratch. They are the bee's knees! I highly recommend trying them out when you have the chance.

4. When Steve Jobs introduced the first iPhone at Macworld in 2007, he all but gave the stylus the finger, saying "Who wants a stylus? You have to get them and put them away, you lose them, yecch!"

5. "Mary Anne with the Shaky Hand" was a song by Pete Townshend, released on The Who's 1967 album, The Who Sell Out.

6. Roam, Dan. *The Back of the Napkin: Solving Problems and Selling Ideas with Pictures.* New York, NY. Penguin Group. 2008.

7. Zull, James. *The Art of Changing the Brain: Enriching the Practice of Teaching by Exploring the Biology of Learning.* Steerling, VA. Stylus Publishing. 2002

8. *Mirrors in the brain: How our minds share actions and emotions.* Rizzolatti, Giacomo; Sinigaglia, Corrado; Anderson, Frances (Trans) New York, NY, US: Oxford University Press. (2008). xiii 242 pp.

CHAPTER 4

1. There are many variations on the basic visual alphabet, with minor variations in basic characters. I crafted these from my experiences with Sunni Brown and David Sibbet, as well as years of creating "Good Enough" drawing tutorial blog posts that broke down complex drawing into simple shapes for anyone to create.

2. Daphne Maurer, Thanujeni Pathman, Catherine J. Mondloch, The shape of boubas: sound–shape correspondences in toddlers and adults, *Developmental Science*, Volume 9, Issue 3, pages 316–322, May 2006

3. http://www.synesthesiatest.org/blog/bouba-kiki-effect

4. Sibbet, David. *Visual Meetings: How Graphics, Sticky Notes and Idea Mapping Can Transform Group Productivity*, Hoboken, NJ. Wiley & Sons, Inc. 2010

5. American theoretical biologist and complex systems researcher Stuart Kauffman coined the term, "the adjacent possible, from his studies about the origin of life on Earth. The term refers to the untapped potential of what could be.

6. My all-time favorite telling of this tale can be found in T.H. White's fantastic book, *The Once and Future King*.

7. Dan Roam nailed this process in his brilliant book, *The Back of The Napkin: Solving Problems and Selling Ideas with Pictures.*

8. Roam, Dan. *The Back of the Napkin: Solving Problems and Selling Ideas with Pictures.* New York, NY. Penguin Group. 2008

9. SoulCollage® facilitator Sherry Eberwein says this at every workshop she holds. I think it applies to visual conversations as well!

CHAPTER 5

1. Want to know how I overcome this fear? In a way, it's like when I purchased my last new car: I freaked out about getting a ding in it—until I got a ding in it. Then I no longer had to protect my perfect new car from getting dinged, so I could relax about where I parked and have more fun with my car. So now, I overcome my fear by "dinging" my blank page: I draw a mark on the page. Any mark. It could be the first line of a title, it could be a squiggle or a swirl. Whatever it is, I simply draw something to break the pure white of that blank page. This simple mark takes the pressure off of drawing perfectly on that blank page because the surface is now imperfect and something I can draw on without "ruining" it. When I notice that people are feeling nervous about picking up the pen and drawing with me on this blank page, I have us all put our "dings" on the page. It gets people drawing, and it gives people permission to make their mark on that blank surface!

2. If you haven't read David Sibbet's book, *Visual Meetings*, get a copy and do so. It is a great resource!

3. People typically experience time in a linear fashion, so we tend to speak and tell stories in a linear fashion: "First this happened, and then that happened, and then this other thing happened." When we break from this linear fashion of speaking or storytelling, we engage in a non-linear perception of time, which feels a bit foreign and confusing to the people we may be speaking with. ("Wait: did you graduate high school and THEN learn how to walk, or did you learn how to walk and then graduated high school?) If you are interested in learning more about the linear and non-linear perceptions of time, Stephen Hawking's classic book, *A Brief History of Time*, is a fascinating starting place! (I am fascinated by this sort of stuff!)

4. What is my favorite tool for diagramming businesses? The Business Model Canvas, of course! You can download a free copy of the Canvas at http://www.businessmodelgeneration.com/downloads/business_model_canvas_poster.pdf.

5. Our brains LOVE metaphor! When we say that something "is like" something else, we are supporting our brain's ability to connect new information with existing knowledge. Drawing these metaphors out for people only serve to strengthen our ability to retain and recall what we are learning. For more information on this topic, check out James Zull's fantastic book, *The Art of Changing the Brain*. (Yes, I am a brain geek!)

6. For more on the power of mandalas, Carl Jung's classic papers on the subject in his book, *Mandala Symbolism*.

7. To learn more about the Business Model Canvas, visit http://www.businessmodelgeneration.com/.

8. To learn more about using the Empathy Map, read the books *Gamestorming* and/or *Business Model Generation* (both found in the Resources section). If you don't want to read, you can watch my short video blog post on the topic at http://jeannelking.com/how-to-use-an-empathy-map-to-understand-your-target-market/.

9. To learn more, visit Tony's website at www.tonybuzan.com.

10. A fantastic book! Check this book's Resources section for details.

11. A Gantt chart is a type of bar chart that displays the amount of work done—or steps still to be taken—for the successful completion of a project.

12. For more information, read Dan's essential book, *The Back of the Napkin*.

13. For more information, read Patti's book, *Drawing Solutions: How Visual Goal Setting Will Change Your Life*. Better yet, visit upyourcreativegenius.com and download your free template!

14. Walt Disney implemented the use of storyboards back in the 1930's for his illustrators to use for shaping the flow of a visual story. Prior to Walt, cartoons had no real plots or stories to move them along: they were mostly entertaining images that moved. Walt was committed to telling stories through his animated films, and the storyboard helped illustrators and writers alike build the linear progression of what would happen: "first this, then that, then this, then the punch line!" The biography, *Walt Disney: An American Original*, provides a fascinating glimpse into this and all the other animation innovations that came from Walt's brain. (It is one of my favorite books!)

15. Venn, J. (July 1880). "On the diagrammatic and mechanical representation of propositions and reasonings". *Philosophical Magazine and Journal of Science*. 5 10 (59): 1–18.

CHAPTER 6

1. "Perfectly," of course, being a relative term! What is perfect to them may not be perfect to me. (Hush up, there, inner critic! If everyone else thinks the conversation worked out perfectly, then that is a bonafide Good Enough visual conversation!)

2. My dad started me on piano lessons when I was a toddler, and over the years I expanded from the piano to the pipe organ, clarinet, alto saxophone, violin, and sousaphone. (This last one was for marching band purposes only.) To this day I am more musical than visual.

3. Miles Davis was a trumpeter, composer, bandleader, and arguably one of the most influential jazz musicians of the 20th century. If you have never heard him play, listen to his album, *Kind of Blue*, and prepare to have your mind blown.

4. I grew up in a silent movie theater in San Francisco. From the time I was four years old until the time I was a "too cool for school" teenager, my family and I would spend our weekends at the Avenue Theater on Silver Avenue.

5. This skill really comes down to two things: practice, and trusting your gut. The more visual conversations you host, the better you will be able to hear what is emerging as a need for the visual conversation. And the better you get at hearing what is emerging, the more you will need to trust your gut that you really are hearing and sensing these things correctly. Don't second-guess yourself—your gut response is usually the right one to follow!

6. Our friend, Shawn Bagheri, of Prospect Rug Gallery in La Jolla, shared this explanation with us.

7. Ah, yes. My "jackass" moment!

8. When I do this, my sketches are really rough and just Good Enough for me to get the design and layout concepts in place. Don't worry about creating a work of art, here! Use your drawing as a planning tool more than anything else.

9. Online searchable databases such as Google Images, the Noun Project, and Yossarian are fantastic ways to spark visual ideas for the concepts you may be working with during the conversation. More are emerging all the time, so experiment and find the resource that works best for you.

10. Come on. Who ever wants to admit that they didn't understand or follow something said in a conversation? When you ask clarifying questions, you are actually doing the entire group a favor!

11. I got this idea from my friend, Melissa Wahl, who would to refer to donuts as "theory food": In theory, it seems like a good idea to eat the donut, but it never tastes as good as you think it will.

CHAPTER 7

1. When we change the language we use to describe a thing, we change how we experience, think about and act toward the thing. For a fascinating look into this idea, check out Economist Keith Chen's 2012 TED talk, "Could Your Language Affect Your Ability To Save Money?"

2. This is otherwise known as "Maslow's Hammer," from Abraham Maslow's 1966 publication, *The Psychology of Science*. (Thank you, psychology degree!)

3. To learn more about "group-think," check out Irving Janis' classic book, *Groupthink: Psychological Studies of Policy Decisions and Fiascos*.

4. To learn more about how to craft powerful questions, read *The Art of Powerful Questions: Catalyzing Insight, Innovation and Action*, by Eric E. Vogt, Juanita Brown, and David Isaacs.

5. Some people keep their laptops or electronic devices open and running because they are taking notes from the conversation on the device. If this will be the case in your visual conversation, it may be helpful to acknowledge that the laptop is being used for note-taking purposes, and that the person using it is truly keying in to the conversation.

6. I have taken a page from social media and ask people to participate in the "phone stack." This is when we all put our phones face-down on the table. The first person that reaches for his or her phone (in an out-of-conversation context) gets to buy everyone lunch!

7. You may have noticed that the illustrations in this book are not perfect. Clearly, my drawings are not all Pablo like Picasso. They work, though. So will yours!

8. Did I mention that I am a brain geek? When taking coursework for my psychology degree, I focused on cognitive psychology and industrial/organizational psychology: I am fascinated by how the brain works, and how the brain works at work.

9. Kolb, David. *Experiential Learning: Experience as the Source of Learning and Development*. Upper Saddle River, NJ. Prentice Hall, Inc. 1984

10. These were originally introduced in Dan's previously-mentioned book, *The Back of the Napkin: Solving Problems and Selling Ideas with Pictures*.

11. If you don't know about SoulPancake, and you like to engage in juicy conversations around Life's Big Questions, then you need to check out their website at www.soulpancake.com! (My hat is off to Rainn Wilson for founding this company. It is brilliant.)

12. Adapted from *The Psychology of Color at Retail*: http://blog.birdsonggregory.com/blog/voice/the-psychology-of-color-at-retail

13. "No es bueno" means "not good" in Spanish.

CHAPTER 8

1. Jonny's charming personality, artisan coffee roasts and world-famous margaritas don't hurt, either!

2. Don't get me wrong: as a graphic facilitator, I am a huge fan of facilitation processes. What I am not a fan of, however, is the "expert" or "outsider" role we may slip into—by assignment or by default. Think about facilitation the way my friend and colleague Eris Weaver uses it: to make things easier. Our goal as visual conversation hosts is to create this state of ease for others.

3. This was also one of the best compliments I have ever received, by the way!

4. This process initially took form as I wrote my master's thesis on the Art of Hosting a nonprofit organization. It has since evolved and been refined with time and experience into what I am sharing with you today.

5. As an example, if you were speaking to a doctor about the state of health insurance, she may talk about how broken the entire system is and how the whole thing should just be scrapped. ("It sucks, it's broken! There are so many problems!") However, if you speak with that same person as the parent of a child who requires medical care, their experience of the system may be more thankful for what the system provides their child, and more open to possibilities and opportunities for making the system work better for other kids and parents. ("Thank goodness for insurance! Our son's procedure would have cost so much more without it. You know, they really should look at changing the way they have parents complete the forms because . . .")

6. I cannot recommend *The Art of Powerful Questions* highly enough as a resource for learning, well, the Art of crafting powerful questions! See the Resources section for details.

7. Did this just make you a little bit nervous? Inviting folks who are not like you? What in the world will happen in this conversation, right? Remember: the way we show up is the way everyone around us gets to show up. Be clear on your conversation's purpose, extend a warm invitation to all, and set the example of how to show up in the space, and you might be pleasantly surprised by the conversation that ensues!

8. They are drawing this conversation along with you, thanks in part to those mirror neurons back in Chapter 3!

9. The essence of this "sauce" comes from my Art of Hosting practice, where one hosts ones self in order to host others. For more information about the Art of Hosting, visit artofhosting.org.

10. These four pieces have emerged as essential to me from my years of designing and hosting World Café conversations with communities, companies, and youth in education. For more information about World Café, visit www.theworldcafe.com.

11. Sometimes I will literally create a "baggage check" station where we can write our assumptions and baggage we want to leave outside of the conversation onto sticky notes and proceed without them. When we're ready to leave, we can choose to pick them back up or let them go.

12. Remember, the way we show up is how everyone else in the room gets to show up. When shining a light on potentially sensitive topics, be mindful in your approach to how this may be for the other person. Shine the light in a way where folks may receive the information and respond to it, rather than pounding it with a hammer and having people react to it.

13. This is another reason why I no longer "do meetings," but instead "host visual conversations." What we are starting to talk about here really touches on bringing a level of trust, understanding, compassion, and empathy to our processes. More times than not, these qualities naturally show up in our conversations that matter than our meetings that matter.

14. To learn more about Dee Hock's theory, read his book, *Birth of the Chaordic Age*.

15. Wear rubber-soled shoes, because you are going to want a firm footing in each of these areas and they are going to be constantly moving beneath you. (Metaphorically speaking, of course!)

CHAPTER 9

1. Sam Kaner, Ph. D. is widely regarded as one of the United States' leading experts in consensus decision-making. (He literally wrote the book about it!) To learn more about him, visit http://www.communityatwork.com/staff.html

2. Kaner, Sam. *The Facilitator's Guide to Participatory Decision-Making*. San Francisco, CA. Jossey-Bass.

3. When I am hosting a visual conversation and someone starts to repeat a point, I use the drawing of the conversation as a focus point, saying "I see we've got that idea captured right over here. Is it complete or does something need to be added?" Most of the time, the person says "Oh! That's right. No, that's it" and the conversation moves on.

4. Dessert usually involves some form of ice cream, in case you were wondering.

5. My master's thesis contributed grounded theory towards the Art of Hosting as a facilitation practice and an operating system for nonprofit organizations. Art of Hosting steward Tenneson Wolfe served as my advisor during this project, and the experience fundamentally shaped my beliefs around how groups and organizations could work. You can read it at www.jeannelking.com/resources/artofhosting.

6. Thank you, amazing brain! Our mirror neurons made the visual conversation's drawings "ours," and now we have a deeper and richer experience (or prior knowledge) to tie new knowledge to. When we revisit the results of that work, our brain gets to unpack those memories at a physical and emotional level, and we "relive" the experience captured in the drawing.

7. The Art of Hosting has deeply shaped my approach to visual conversations. For more information about the Art of Hosting and related practices, visit www.artofhosting.org.

8. Check out Chris' website at www.chriscorrigan.com. The man does inspiring work, and he is deep!

9. Metaphorically speaking, of course. To my knowledge, Chris has not pranced about in tights during an Art of Hosting gathering. (And if he has, I want to see pictures!)

10. If you have worked with me on a project, you know that in my book EVERYTHING comes down to the true purpose for the event or conversation. If we are out of alignment with our intended purpose, we are not standing on a solid foundation. Worse, the folks we invite to join us can "smell" that something is not quite right between what we said we were doing and what we are actually doing. In order to be an effective visual conversationalist, the integrity of your conversations must be preserved. Preserve the integrity of your purpose and the conversation's integrity is off to a great start!

11. This is your opportunity to be the Host or Hostess with the Most or Mostest!

Acknowledgements

You know that moment when someone wins an Oscar and they are on stage fumbling inside their jacket for the huge list of people they want to thank because they have only got 30 seconds and about a million people to honor and they don't want to miss any of them because the impact they have had on this person's life has been profound, even in ways they may not even realize?

This is exactly what it feels like to write the acknowledgements section of a book! I am so worried that I will forget to mention someone who truly deserves it, so let's just start with a blanket statement:

I am tremendously grateful to EVERYONE who made this book even possible. I am truly honored and humbled by your encouragement and support, and there are not enough words in the WORLD to express how thankful I am to each and every one of you.

In particular, and in no particular order, I want to say thank you to:

Lestat's on Park for helping me write with great music, great space, and lots of Nick's SBA lattes

Jerry Guern for the fellow-writer support and accountability

Elle Brooks for helping me dissolve editing obstacles with love and laughter

Diane Bleck, Felena Hanson, and Karie Kaufmann for encouraging me to be bigger and to claim the space I needed to make it so

Annette Mason and Poppy Fitch for expanding my thinking and inspiring me on the regular

Rebecca Tall Brown for so many things there simply aren't enough words

April Elliot Kent for being a good enough friend to pat my hand with a smile and say "oh honey," when I declared that I was going to turn my first-draft manuscript into a finished book for publication in a month

The whole online crew who responded to a survey when I was massively stuck and needed a shift in thinking, including but not limited to: **Manual Frias, Mauro Toselli, Dara Bilow, Eileen Piersa, Christy Pavano-Heiskala, Meridith Gronroos, Bob McGrath, Kylie Dunn, Igor Goldkind, Ellie Pope, Nikki Haritatos, Kristin Stewart, Sunny BenBelkacem, Roberta Faulhaber, Dora Rowe, Anne McColl, Leah Silverman, Claire Holgate, Mike Rohde, Roy Blumenthal, Tracey Levasseur, Dominik De Buyser, Michael Carroll, Bob te Riele, Piotr Poznański, Natalia Luptakova, Kevin Dulle, Marliese Bartz, Phenella Lill, Angeline Veeneman, and Melynda Benlemlih**

Michelle Boos-Stone and Paul Hong for saying exactly what I needed to hear right when I needed to hear it

The Art of Hosting community for always opening my eyes, expanding my mind and pushing my edges

Chris Corrigan for extending an invitation that changed my life

Dan Roam for writing a book that changed my life

Anthony Robbins for embodying permission to change my life

Ken Blanchard for showing me how to lead with love and spread the happy

Sunni Brown for being my first teacher in the graphic facilitation world, and for inspiring me to imagine a bigger journey for myself

All the visual conversationalists out there who pick up the pen, share the love and spread the word

Silvia Mah and Kathleen Clark for being my manuscript's eyes when I could no longer see

Rachel Kowalski for helping me use my words mo bettah

DesignGood for making my baby look all pretty

Janine Herling for inviting me to walk on her side of the street

Jamie Lawson for loving me and being—hands-down—the most patient man on the planet

About the Author

If Dan Roam and Anthony Robbins had a love-child, it would be Jeannel King.

Jeannel has a passion for drawing forth the best in ourselves and each other.

A recovering nonprofit executive, King decided long ago to stop "having meetings" and start "hosting visual conversations." As a graphic facilitator and Stick Figure Strategist®, Jeannel designs and hosts visual conversations for startup companies to elite Special Forces units, and everything in between. Her visual processes generate greater clarity, deeper understanding, more engaged teams and exceptional results for her clients.

Her popular first eBook, What You Draw Is Good Enough, convinces people around the world to pick up the pen and have fun drawing out ideas. Translated into Spanish and Czech, this book helps readers reconnect with the part of themselves that used to love drawing when they were kids, and to bring more of that fun-loving and creative part of themselves to all that they do.

Jeannel enjoys speaking publicly to share her passion—and pass the pen—for drawing out ideas while drawing forth the best in ourselves and each other at venues worldwide.

Jeannel holds degrees in psychology and nonprofit management, and is a past-president of the International Forum of Visual Practitioners. Her facilitation practice is grounded in such models as the Art of Hosting, Appreciative Inquiry and World Cafe.

Jeannel lives with her boyfriend, Jamie, and kitten, Wilhelmina Crabbycakes, in San Diego. She's a bit embarrassed about how much she loves ethnic food, blogging, animation and forced-creativity reality TV shows.

You can learn more about Jeannel at www.jeannelking.com.

CPSIA information can be obtained
at www.ICGtesting.com
Printed in the USA
LVHW111001061121
702607LV00011B/285

9 780990 786405